Cambridge Elements

Elements in Language Teaching
edited by
Heath Rose
University of Oxford
Jim McKinley
University College London

INFORMAL DIGITAL LEARNING OF ENGLISH

Ju Seong Lee
The Education University of Hong Kong

Shaftesbury Road, Cambridge CB2 8EA, United Kingdom

One Liberty Plaza, 20th Floor, New York, NY 10006, USA

477 Williamstown Road, Port Melbourne, VIC 3207, Australia

314–321, 3rd Floor, Plot 3, Splendor Forum, Jasola District Centre, New Delhi – 110025, India

103 Penang Road, #05–06/07, Visioncrest Commercial, Singapore 238467

Cambridge University Press is part of Cambridge University Press & Assessment, a department of the University of Cambridge.

We share the University's mission to contribute to society through the pursuit of education, learning and research at the highest international levels of excellence.

www.cambridge.org
Information on this title: www.cambridge.org/9781009641685
DOI: 10.1017/9781009641647

© Ju Seong Lee 2026

This publication is in copyright. Subject to statutory exception and to the provisions of relevant collective licensing agreements, no reproduction of any part may take place without the written permission of Cambridge University Press & Assessment.

When citing this work, please include a reference to the DOI 10.1017/9781009641647

First published 2026

A catalogue record for this publication is available from the British Library

A Cataloging-in-Publication data record for this Element is available from the Library of Congress

ISBN 978-1-009-64167-8 Hardback
ISBN 978-1-009-64168-5 Paperback
ISSN 2632-4415 (online)
ISSN 2632-4407 (print)

Cambridge University Press & Assessment has no responsibility for the persistence or accuracy of URLs for external or third-party internet websites referred to in this publication and does not guarantee that any content on such websites is, or will remain, accurate or appropriate.

For EU product safety concerns, contact us at Calle de José Abascal, 56, 1°, 28003 Madrid, Spain, or email eugpsr@cambridge.org

Informal Digital Learning of English

Elements in Language Teaching

DOI: 10.1017/9781009641647
First published online: January 2026

Ju Seong Lee
The Education University of Hong Kong

Author for correspondence: Ju Seong Lee, jslee@eduhk.hk

Abstract: As globalization spreads, English has become a lingua franca. Emerging technologies (e.g., Artificial Intelligence) now make learning English more accessible, affordable, and tailored to each learner. Social media and digital platforms immerse users in English, offering interactive, personalized, and engaging experiences that fuel Informal Digital Learning of English (IDLE). Research spanning more than ten regions has found that IDLE brings a wide range of benefits, including greater motivation, higher academic achievement, and stronger speaking skills. Today, IDLE is being woven into schools and local communities through partnerships among teachers, NGOs, and industry leaders. This volume seeks to (a) showcase the latest research on IDLE, (b) highlight examples of IDLE in educational and community settings, and (c) chart future pathways for practice, research, and collaboration.

Keywords: informal digital learning of English; IDLE; social impact; researcher–teacher collaboration; trans-disciplinary collaboration; AI

© Ju Seong Lee 2026

ISBNs: 9781009641678 (HB), 9781009641685 (PB), 9781009641647 (OC)
ISSNs: 2632-4415 (online), 2632-4407 (print)

Contents

1 Overview   1

2 Informal Digital Learning of English   5

3 Antecedents and Consequences of IDLE   20

4 Bringing IDLE into Schools and Communities   37

5 Future Directions for IDLE   51

   References   58

1 Overview

Motivation for this Element

Informal Digital Learning of English (IDLE) refers to how learners autonomously engage with English across digital spaces, outside of the traditional classroom (Lee, 2022a). Coincidentally, the term "IDLE" sounds like *aideul*, the Korean word for "children," which captures the spirit of how young learners naturally acquire language – through curiosity, creativity, and playful experimentation in online environments. My own journey with English began in much this way. As a seventh grader, I fell in love with "real" English through music, movies, and sports. By high school, I found myself shedding my anxiety and imagining life in English-speaking settings. In my twenties, IDLE gave me the skills and confidence to explore more than ten different countries, whether studying, backpacking, volunteering, or working abroad.

Seeing the potential of IDLE to spark motivation and growth, I introduced these strategies to my Korean students in my early thirties. Yet, weaving IDLE into classroom life was far from simple. Many students, parents, colleagues, and senior teachers hesitated, their uncertainty rooted in Korea's strong group-oriented culture and intense focus on exams – especially at my school, where such societal pressures ran deep (Lee, 2020a; Zadorozhnyy et al., 2025). My perspective widened further when, after four years of teaching in Korea, I encountered Moroccan learners who spoke English with remarkable fluency and confidence – thanks to IDLE (Dressman & Lee, 2021). Through interviews, observations, and consultations, I witnessed firsthand how powerfully IDLE could shape English learning and use beyond traditional classrooms (Lee & Dressman, 2018).

Today, IDLE has become a global phenomenon, fueled by affordable smartphones and the widespread reach of platforms, such as Meta (formerly Facebook), Instagram, YouTube, and Netflix (Dressman et al., 2023; Soyoof et al., 2023; Liu et al., 2025). This Element explores how changing global trends and rapid technological advancements have made IDLE possible, how it supports language learning, and how partnerships are helping to weave it into schools and communities.

Background and Context

In our rapidly changing, interconnected world, English has become a vital tool for global communication (Graddol, 2006; Crystal, 2010). It brings together people from diverse cultures, fosters international collaboration, and opens doors to global conversations (Warschauer, 2000;

Friedman, 2005). Recent technological breakthroughs – especially in generative Artificial Intelligence – are revolutionizing English learning, making it more accessible, affordable, and adaptable to every learner's needs (Godwin-Jones, 2022; Liu et al., 2024a; Lai & Sundqvist, 2025).

Digital platforms now offer learners vivid, authentic English experiences (Liu & Darvin, 2023). Interactive apps and vast online courses, alongside dynamic social media, allow users to practice English in real time – participating in discussions, sharing interests, and immersing themselves in multimedia content (Lee, Y.-J., 2023). Apps, such as Babbel and Duolingo, use AI to personalize lessons, while communities on Twitter and Reddit let learners converse with people around the world about topics they care about (Chik & Ho, 2017; Isbell, 2018; Godwin-Jones, 2021; Smith et al., 2024).

Within this dynamic landscape, more and more language learners are turning to informal digital methods to strengthen their English (Sockett, 2014; Richards, 2015; Sundqvist & Sylvén, 2016; Toffoli, 2020; Toffoli et al., 2023). IDLE marks a shift from traditional, classroom-based learning to a more self-directed, technology-driven approach (Lee, 2022a; Dressman et al., 2023). Learners take charge, exploring a wealth of online resources – YouTube tutorials, podcasts, language exchanges – at their own pace and according to their unique interests (Rezai & Goodarzi, 2025).

Similar concepts, such as Extramural English (Sundqvist, 2009; Sundqvist & Sylvén, 2016) and Online Informal Learning of English (Sockett, 2014; Toffoli & Sockett, 2015), highlight this evolving landscape. Researchers are uncovering how activities such as gaming, social media engagement, and digital content creation effectively support language learning well beyond the classroom (Sundqvist, 2009, 2019, 2022, 2024; Chik, 2014; Sockett, 2014; Lai, 2017; Dressman & Sadler, 2020; Reinders et al., 2022; Toffoli et al., 2023). Systematic reviews and meta-analyses synthesize these findings, offering a broad view of IDLE's influence (Dizon, 2023; Guo & Lee, 2023; Soyoof et al., 2023; Guan et al., 2024; Aiju et al., 2025; Dressman et al., 2025; Kusyk et al., 2025). Special journal issues and dedicated symposia further spotlight the latest research and foster a vibrant community of scholars and practitioners (Sylvén & Sundqvist, 2017; Arndt & Lyrigkou, 2019; Sauro & Zourou, 2019; Reynolds & Teng, 2021; Lee & Chik, 2025; Lee et al., 2026).

As research increasingly highlights IDLE's positive effects (e.g., improved proficiency and motivation), researchers are also uncovering the factors that drive learners to embrace these practices (Guan et al., 2024;

Zadorozhnyy & Lee, 2024; see Section 3). Understanding what motivates learners and how they interact with technology enables educators to design IDLE activities that blend smoothly with formal curricula (Melnyk & Morrison-Beedy, 2012; Lai & Lee, 2024; Lee & Chik, 2025). By aligning IDLE with educational goals, teachers can make learning more engaging, effective, and expansive (Dressman et al., 2023; Lee, 2024).

Recently, IDLE has moved from theory to practice; it is now used in classrooms, built into curricula, embedded in AI-powered language apps, and woven into community projects (Dressman & Lee, 2021; Lee et al., 2025; Rezai et al., 2025). These initiatives thrive on transdisciplinary collaboration, connecting experts in education, technology, linguistics, psychology, and sociology (Melnyk & Morrison-Beedy, 2012; Arndt et al., 2022; Lee, 2024). For example, partnerships between researchers and industry have produced AI-mediated IDLE programs that personalize learning beyond the classroom (Lee et al., 2025). In line with the UN's Sustainable Development Goal 4 (lifelong learning), community projects are also using informal strategies to support language learning among marginalized and under-resourced groups, helping them adapt and thrive in new societies (Sundqvist, 2022; Reinders and Lee, 2023; Lee, 2024; see Section 4).

As the field of IDLE continues to expand, this Element looks to the future (see Section 5). Our aim is to explore how IDLE can further enrich language learning – by including more diverse learners and contexts, extending IDLE to languages beyond English, deepening research with new theories and tools, and refining methods to strengthen evidence. Ultimately, we hope to help educators and communities integrate IDLE meaningfully, maximizing its benefits for learners everywhere (Dizon, 2023; Liu et al., 2024).

1.1 The Aim and Structure of This Element

This Element unfolds across five sections, each designed to guide readers through the evolving landscape of IDLE:

Section 1: Overview
The opening section lays the foundation for the entire volume. It delves into the motivation behind the Element, provides essential background, and sets the stage for what follows. Readers will find a clear outline of the Element's overall aims, along with a roadmap previewing Sections 2 through 5.

Section 2: IDLE
This section places IDLE within the sweeping changes brought about by globalization and technological advances from the 1990s to the 2020s. It discusses why IDLE is so relevant today, introducing four core principles – formality, location, pedagogy, and locus of control – that define its character. Further, the section breaks down IDLE into four distinct learning spaces, forming the backbone of the IDLE Continuum Model, a practical framework for teachers aiming to bring IDLE into formal classrooms. The discussion also contrasts IDLE with traditional English education and examines related concepts, such as Extramural English and Online Informal Learning of English. In addition, the section reviews key literature and recent trends, offering a holistic and up-to-date understanding of IDLE's rapid expansion (Sundqvist, 2009; Sockett, 2014; Toffoli & Sockett, 2015; Lee, 2022a).

Section 3: Antecedents and Consequences of IDLE
Drawing on a wide array of empirical research, this section maps out both the precursors and outcomes of IDLE engagement. A comprehensive visual model illustrates these relationships, providing researchers and educators with a clear picture of what is already known about IDLE – and what remains to be explored. This section also serves as a practical guide, enabling the design of evidence-based IDLE interventions tailored to the needs of specific schools or communities.

Section 4: Bringing IDLE into Schools and Communities
As the evidence base for IDLE grows, so too does the call to embed it in formal education. This section begins with a candid look at the challenges faced in integrating IDLE into school systems in places such as Hong Kong and Indonesia. It introduces the IDLE Continuum Model, which gives educators at every level – K-12 and higher education – a flexible framework for blending IDLE into their curricula, supported by conceptual, empirical, and experimental research. Practical pedagogical strategies are discussed, showing how educators can transition smoothly across different modes of digital learning: from formal and non-formal settings to extracurricular and extramural experiences. The vital role of teachers – as context experts who understand both research and the unique needs of their students and institutions – is underscored. In alignment with the Research Excellence Framework's emphasis on social impact, the section highlights how IDLE initiatives have reached beyond academia into communities, engaging stakeholders such as teachers,

NGOs, government officials, and industry partners. It also introduces the "Care–Innovation–Sustainability Model" and illustrates how multidisciplinary teams have applied this model to IDLE implementation in Indonesian schools and communities.

Section 5: Future Directions for IDLE
Building on the cutting-edge research presented in Sections 1–4, the final section looks ahead to the future of IDLE. It charts pathways for expanding IDLE to more diverse learners and contexts – including young students and those in the Global South – and for embracing Languages Other Than English (LOTE), such as Korean and Chinese. The section explores how IDLE can be deepened by drawing on various theoretical frameworks, including ecological systems theory and the technology acceptance model. It encourages methodological innovation, whether through digital learner analytics or by adopting research approaches from other disciplines, such as experience sampling methods (ESM). Innovative strategies for integrating IDLE into schools are discussed, always with an eye on local contexts. Finally, the section advocates for IDLE as a tool for broader social impact, aiming to reach more learners and communities in alignment with the United Nations Sustainable Development Goals – particularly SDG 3 (health and well-being) and SDG 4 (quality education).

2 Informal Digital Learning of English

2.1 The Rise of Digital Technology and English Learning

What might be contributing to the global surge in IDLE among young English learners (Guo & Lee, 2023; Guan et al., 2024)? A key factor appears to be the ongoing progression of digital innovation and the increasing accessibility of advanced technologies (Soyoof et al., 2023). Over time, technological developments have likely reshaped how learners engage with English, as illustrated in Figure 1. Drawing on research that traces the evolution of Computer-Assisted Language Learning (CALL; Warschauer, 2004; Chun, 2016, 2019; Sauro & Zourou, 2019; Lee, 2022a), this section outlines a tentative timeline of digital shifts and their potential influence on English learning, suggesting that technology has, in many cases, extended language learning beyond the traditional classroom. Since the 1990s, each decade seems to have introduced notable changes in language acquisition, gradually lowering barriers and expanding possibilities.

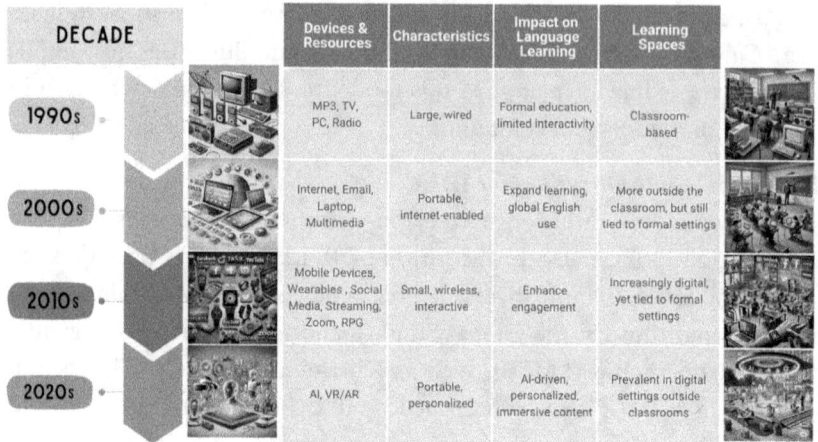

Figure 1 Digital Technology and English Learning: A Chronological Evolution

The 1990s: Wired and Walled in
In the 1990s, learning was often tied to bulky, wired devices – MP3 players, satellite TV boxes, and desktop computers – primarily available in wealthier, developed regions (Stockwell, 2008). English instruction largely remained within conventional classrooms, shaped by fixed curricula and limited digital tools. Authentic English content – such as podcasts, films, or global media – was not widely accessible outside school, meaning students typically depended on textbooks and teacher guidance (Kim, 2015).

The 2000s: Portability and Early Connections
With the turn of the millennium came a wave of educational change. Portable devices such as laptops and early tablets began to loosen the spatial constraints of learning (Kim, 2015). The internet and email introduced learners to a broader array of English-language materials and intercultural interactions (Nah et al., 2008). Still, access to these tools was uneven. While some households in affluent areas such as northern Europe came online, the benefits were often limited to those with sufficient resources, reinforcing existing digital divides (McCallum & Tafazoli, 2024).

The 2010s: On-the-Go Learning and Creative Autonomy
The 2010s marked the proliferation of smartphones, smartwatches, and social media platforms such as YouTube, Instagram, and TikTok, which arguably reduced the constraints of time and place (Chik & Ho, 2017; Godwin-Jones, 2021). Lightweight, wireless devices enabled learners to turn idle moments – on public transport, in cafés, or at the gym – into

potential learning opportunities (Reinders & Benson, 2017). Learners increasingly moved beyond passive consumption, producing their own content – memes, vlogs, and tutorials – aligned with their interests (Godwin-Jones, 2016; Chen, 2020). This period may have fostered greater learner agency, allowing individuals to shape their English learning paths outside traditional publishing structures (Benson, 2011a, 2011b).

The 2020s: Immersive and Personalized Experiences
Emerging technologies such as AI, VR, and AR are once again reshaping the landscape of language learning (Lin & Lan, 2015; Kaplan-Rakowski et al., 2021). Generative AI can offer lessons tailored to individual learner profiles, while VR and AR simulate immersive English-speaking environments – virtual cafés, international conferences, or bustling cityscapes (Godwin-Jones, 2022; Stockwell & Wang, 2025). Increasingly affordable and multifunctional devices may be helping to bridge geographic gaps, enabling real-time collaboration across borders (Dooly & Sadler, 2013; Lee & Song, 2020). These tools appear to blur the line between formal instruction and informal exploration, potentially supporting fluency through experiential learning (Dressman et al., 2023).

IDLE's Bright Future: Learners in Control
This ongoing technological evolution seems to be positioning IDLE as a prominent mode of English learning. As digital tools become more adaptive, accessible, and embedded in daily life, learners may be gaining more autonomy over their language development (Lai, 2017; Jeon, 2022; Lai & Lee, 2024). IDLE offers alternatives to rigid curricula, suggesting more flexible and personalized pathways to proficiency in a world where English increasingly mediates global communication (Benson, 2011b; Reinders & Benson, 2017; Lee, 2022a). Nonetheless, digital inequality continues to constrain access for some. The future of language learning may well unfold not only in classrooms but also across the expansive, digitally connected environments that many learners now navigate daily (Warschauer, 2000; UNICEF, 2020; Sundqvist, 2022; Lee et al., 2025).

2.2 From Classrooms to IDLE: Redefining Language Learning Spaces

For decades, second language acquisition research focused on what happens inside learners' minds – memory capacity, motivation levels, innate aptitude (Papi & Hiver, 2025). But this cognitive approach overlooked a crucial element: the real-world actions learners take to master a language.

"Proactive Language Learning Theory" changes the game by spotlighting four key behaviors that drive success (Papi & Hiver, 2025):

1. *Input-seeking* – Surrounding themselves with English through *Netflix* binges, podcast commutes, or social media scrolling (Lee, 2022a; Peng et al., 2025)
2. *Interaction-seeking* – Joining Discord servers, commenting on *TikTok* videos, or voice-chatting in multiplayer games (Sundqvist, 2019; Lee, Y.-J., 2023)
3. *Information-seeking* – Instantaneously consulting *DeepL* for translations or watching YouTube tutorials on tricky grammar points (Cole & Vanderplank, 2016; Arndt & Woore, 2018)
4. *Feedback-seeking* – Submitting *Reddit* posts for native speaker review or using AI writing assistants for real-time corrections (Isbell, 2018; Godwin-Jones, 2022)

This learner-centered perspective perfectly captures today's reality – where smartphones have become more powerful than textbooks, and fluency grows through organic digital immersion rather than rigid classroom drills (Godwin-Jones, 2018, 2019). The rise of IDLE exemplifies this transformation. Consider how modern learners operate (Reinders et al., 2022; Dressman et al., 2023; Lee, 2024): A teenager absorbs colloquial phrases from *Twitch* streams (*input*), debates in *Facebook* groups (*interaction*), researches slang on *Urban Dictionary* (*information*), and refines pronunciation via speech-recognition apps (*feedback*). These behaviors do not just supplement formal education – they are becoming the primary drivers of language acquisition for digital natives (Butler, 2015; Lee, 2022a).

This paradigm shift reflects broader changes in education. As Reinders and Benson (2017) demonstrated, effective learning now happens anywhere – during a morning jog (listening to podcasts), in line at Starbucks (flipping through flashcard apps), or between *Zoom* meetings (chatting with language partners). The four pillars of Language Learning Beyond the Classroom – formality, location, pedagogy, and locus of control – are being supercharged by digital tools that make English acquisition seamless and integrated into daily life (Benson, 2011b; Reinders & Benson, 2017; Lee, 2019):

- **Formality:** Learners craft their own rhythms, ditching rigid timetables to study when inspiration strikes – whether at dawn, during lunch breaks, or late at night.
- **Location:** Parks, coffee shops, subway cars, or cozy bedrooms transform into vibrant learning hubs, untethered from desks and whiteboards.

- **Pedagogy:** Curricula bend to individual passions – gamers master English through strategy guides, K-pop fans dissect lyrics, and aspiring chefs follow international recipes.
- **Locus of Control:** Learners steer their journeys, choosing apps, media, or peer interactions that resonate with their goals, creating bespoke pathways to fluency.

Lee's (2019) IDLE model captures this cultural transformation, showing how digital spaces have evolved into sophisticated learning ecosystems. From algorithm-curated *YouTube* feeds that teach grammar through pop culture, to AI chatbots offering 24/7 conversation practice, today's learners are not just studying English – they are 'living' it (Lee, 2024). As illustrated in Figure 2, these emerging digital learning spaces are not merely alternatives to classrooms; they are becoming the main stage where authentic, motivation-driven language acquisition unfolds (Tsang & Lee, 2023; Rezai et al., 2025). This revolution has given rise to four distinct types of digital learning spaces:

1. **Formal Digital Learning: The Structured Classroom Goes Digital**
   Here, technology serves traditional teaching methods. Smartboards display grammar exercises, students watch preselected *TED Talks*, and computer labs host scripted language software sessions. While these tools modernize the classroom, the teacher remains firmly in control – students might interact with digital content, but within strict curricular

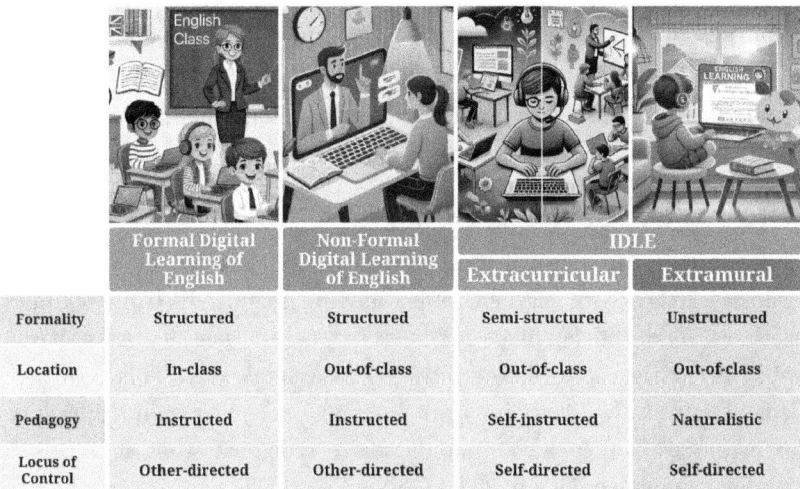

	Formal Digital Learning of English	Non-Formal Digital Learning of English	IDLE	
			Extracurricular	Extramural
Formality	Structured	Structured	Semi-structured	Unstructured
Location	In-class	Out-of-class	Out-of-class	Out-of-class
Pedagogy	Instructed	Instructed	Self-instructed	Naturalistic
Locus of Control	Other-directed	Other-directed	Self-directed	Self-directed

Figure 2 IDLE in Digital Learning Spaces Based on LBC's Four Dimensions

boundaries (Kim, 2015). Think of a class collectively using *Rosetta Stone* under teacher supervision, with every click tracked and assessed.

2. **Non-Formal Digital Learning: Guided Learning Beyond School Walls**
   This middle ground offers structured lessons outside institutional settings (e.g., shadow education; Yung, 2015). A business professional might take scheduled *Zoom* lessons with a Cambridge-certified tutor on *Italki*, or a student could enroll in a self-paced TOEFL prep course on *Udemy*. While more flexible than classroom learning, these options still follow designed syllabi and measurable outcomes – just without school bells or report cards (Yung, 2019).

3. **Extracurricular IDLE: The Bridge between Classrooms and Curiosity**
   Blending formal education with personal exploration, this approach lets learners stretch their wings while maintaining ties to academic goals (Sundqvist & Sylvén, 2016; Sylvén & Sundqvist, 2017; Lee, 2019). Imagine high schoolers completing teacher-assigned *Netflix* viewing logs, university students collaborating on *Google Docs* for group projects, or language app streaks being counted toward course credit (Li, 2018). The activities are chosen by educators, but execution relies on students' independent engagement with digital tools (Hwang & Lai, 2017).

4. **Extramural IDLE: Pure Passion-Driven Learning**
   This is where magic happens organically – gamers coordinating raids in English on *Discord*, K-pop fans translating lyrics for their *Twitter* followers, or binge-watchers absorbing accents from British detective series (Sauro & Zourou, 2019; Vazquez-Calvo et al., 2019). Completely divorced from formal education (Sockett, 2014; Sundqvist & Sylvén, 2016; Sylvén & Sundqvist, 2017; Lee, 2019), these activities thrive on intrinsic motivation. Unlike extracurricular IDLE, there is no teacher looking over shoulders – just learners diving into digital worlds where English becomes the natural currency of connection and enjoyment (Lee, 2022a).

The boundaries between these spaces are increasingly fluid (Bruen & Erdocia, 2024), with learners often moving seamlessly from textbook exercises (*formal*) to language exchange apps (*non-formal*) to meme-sharing with international friends (*extramural*) in a single day. This ecosystem demonstrates how digital environments have not just expanded learning opportunities – they have fundamentally redefined what it means to "study" a language (Dizon, 2023; Guo & Lee, 2023).

In December 2024, the Hong Kong Education Bureau awarded a one-time grant of HK$400,000 to K-12 schools, aiming to strengthen students' English abilities through self-directed learning (Yiu, 2024). The Bureau emphasized that "Language acquisition should not be confined to the classroom, and students also learn through various means...it is important to nurture students' self-directed learning so that they can proactively take charge of their own learning." This move highlights the Hong Kong government's recognition of learning environments beyond the classroom, including digital spaces like IDLE. English teachers are thus encouraged to fully harness these online platforms to help students further develop their English skills (Lee et al., 2024; Lee & Taylor, 2024).

Lee's (2022a) IDLE Continuum Model vividly illustrates this evolving landscape, moving beyond rigid labels to present a fluid spectrum of language learning experiences. Earlier researchers (e.g., Sundqvist & Sylvén, 2016; Sylvén & Sundqvist, 2017; Lee, 2019) drew sharp lines between extracurricular learning (loosely connected to schools) and extramural learning (completely outside institutional reach). By contrast, the IDLE continuum reveals how students can move along a connected pathway – from structured, teacher-supported activities ("weak IDLE") to fully independent, student-driven digital learning in authentic contexts ("strong IDLE"; Lee, 2022a, 2024).

Research highlights this developmental journey. For instance, Zhang and Liu (2022) showed that teachers can play an active role in guiding students as they transition from extracurricular to extramural settings, effectively stretching the classroom's boundaries. Building on this idea, Liu, Guan, Qiu, and Lee (2024) designed a twelve-week IDLE program that carefully increased learner autonomy. The program began with three weeks of teacher-led instruction, then gradually shifted responsibility to students over the following weeks, culminating in high autonomy by the end. Their results revealed that students in the IDLE program grew much more willing to communicate in English than their peers in traditional classes.

Similarly, Rezai et al. (2025) explored the effectiveness of both extra-curricular and extramural IDLE for Iranian EFL university students' reading comprehension. After a four-month intervention, both groups performed significantly better than the control group, with no notable difference between them. These findings suggest that both forms of IDLE provide rich environments for language exposure and reading development. Introducing IDLE even in a classroom-based, teacher-supported format ("weak IDLE") can yield benefits for EFL learners' reading skills that are just as substantial as those achieved through completely independent, extramural IDLE ("strong IDLE").

By reimagining learning spaces in this way, the IDLE model empowers students to take ownership of their language journey. It blends the structure of guided learning with the freedom of personal exploration, allowing learners to engage with English in ways that resonate with their interests and aspirations (Lee, 2022a). This shift makes language learning more dynamic, meaningful, and personalized – offering a fresh perspective on how students can build autonomy, motivation, and real-world communication skills, as explored further in Section 4 (Peng et al., 2022; Lee et al., 2025; Peng et al., 2025).

2.3 IDLE vs. Formal English Education

The notion of the "prosumer" – someone who is both a producer and a consumer – was first introduced by futurist Alvin Toffler in his 1980 book *The Third Wave* (Toffler, 1980). Toffler envisioned a future where people would move beyond passive consumption and play an active part in shaping the goods, services, and media they engage with. This vision has become even more relevant in the digital age, as Don Tapscott (1996, 2008) highlight how technology empowers ordinary users to be creators. Today, anyone can upload videos to YouTube, personalize products, or contribute to open-source projects, becoming active participants in digital culture.

This idea closely aligns with the concept of "participatory culture," where individuals do not just passively consume content, but actively create, share, and interact with media and with each other (Lomicka & Ducate, 2021). In participatory culture, creative expression and civic engagement are open to almost everyone, thanks to low barriers that invite widespread involvement (Jenkins et al., 2009). There is strong encouragement for people not only to make things but also to share their creations widely, fostering an environment of collaboration and exchange. Informal mentorship is common, as experienced participants naturally guide newcomers, passing along what they have learned. People are motivated by a feeling that their contributions matter, and they develop a sense of social connection and community, caring about and responding to what others have made (Jenkins et al., 2009; Sauro, 2017).

In this evolving landscape, the prosumer is not just a recipient but a co-architect of their own experiences, blurring the traditional line between audience and author (Sauro, 2017). This dual identity resonates strongly with receptive and productive IDLE (Lee, 2022a). In receptive IDLE, learners immerse themselves in English-rich environments – streaming *Netflix* thrillers, binge-watching sitcoms, or scrolling through global news feeds – soaking up accents, idioms, and cultural cues (Lee, 2019, 2022a). Productive IDLE, on the other hand, sees learners using language for personal expression: tweeting clever remarks, debating on *Reddit*, writing fanfiction, or coordinating strategies in online games (Lee, 2019, 2022a).

Recent research shows that learners rarely separate receptive and productive IDLE into distinct categories (Lee & Chiu, 2024). Instead, they blend them effortlessly into a rich, continuous learning experience. For instance, someone might binge-watch *Bridgerton* to absorb the rhythm and elegance of British English, then jump onto *Tumblr* to unravel plot twists with fans from around the world – transforming passive viewing into active dialogue (Lee, 2024). Likewise, a *Minecraft* enthusiast might study in-game tutorials to grasp vocabulary and mechanics, then collaborate with Indonesian teammates on *Discord* to plan elaborate builds, turning comprehension into real-time negotiation.

Liu and Lee (2023) also highlight how IDLE offers a unique advantage over conventional classroom methods, which often rely on grammar drills and high-pressure exams. While formal education tends to tether learners to textbooks and rigid assessments, IDLE flourishes in the dynamic terrain of digital culture, where curiosity – not curriculum – fuels engagement. Learners often abandon rote memorization in favor of solving real-world problems, replacing structured lesson plans with spontaneous, self-guided exploration (Soyoof et al., 2024). This shift empowers them to use English not just as a subject to study, but as a living tool for creativity, connection, and personal growth (Lee, 2022a; Dressman et al., 2025; see Table 1 for a detailed contrast).

Table 1 Key Differences between IDLE and Formal English Education

Aspect	IDLE	Formal English Education
Multimodality	Combines videos, audio, games, interactive apps, memes, and social media posts.	Primarily relies on textbooks, worksheets, and printed materials.
Nature	Flexible and driven by personal passions and interests.	Highly structured, following a fixed curriculum.

(*Continued*)

Table 1 (Continued)

Aspect	IDLE	Formal English Education
Content	Real-world media such as YouTube, Instagram, podcasts, and gaming chats.	Prescribed textbooks, grammar drills, and classroom scripts.
Control	Learners choose their own pace, topics, and methods of study.	Teachers set the pace, goals, and deadlines.
Authenticity	Encourages real-life interactions (e.g., online gaming conversations, Twitter threads).	Often relies on scripted role-plays or artificial textbook dialogues.
Risk-taking	Fosters experimentation with slang, accents, and informal expressions.	Rewards "correct" answers, such as grammar and vocabulary tests.
Power dynamics	Peer-driven, with learners collaborating in fan communities or gaming chats.	Teacher-centered, with a clear hierarchy of authority.
Assessment	Rarely graded; focuses on personal growth and self-reflection.	Grades are typically based on high-stakes exams and standardized tests.
Motivation	Intrinsic, personal goals (e.g., writing fan fiction).	External pressures (e.g., grades, certificates).
Inclusivity	Welcomes diverse learning styles, allowing learners to engage in ways that suit them.	Often ranks students by test performance, creating hierarchies.
Stress	Low-pressure, enjoyable, and exploratory.	Can be anxiety-inducing, with an emphasis on avoiding mistakes.
Creativity	Sparks innovation, such as creating memes, videos, or fan fiction.	Follows rigid formats, such as structured essays or test responses.
Lifelong and lifewide learning	Continues naturally beyond formal education, applying skills in workplaces or hobbies.	Often ends after exams or graduation, with limited real-world application.

IDLE stands out because it allows learners to engage with English in authentic, everyday situations (Dressman & Sadler, 2020). On platforms such as *YouTube*, *TikTok*, *Instagram*, and online games, learners are driven by personal interests rather than external pressures such as grades or exams (Godwin-Jones, 2019; Lee et al., 2024). For instance, they might analyze their favorite TV shows, join fan forums to discuss plot twists, or debate trending topics on *Reddit* (Sauro, 2017; Isbell, 2018). This freedom enables learners to choose topics that excite them, explore creative expressions like experimenting with slang or accents, and even create memes (Lee, 2024). Without the stress of grades, learners feel safe to take risks, make mistakes, and grow naturally (Lee & Chiu, 2023; Uztosun & Kök, 2023).

IDLE also goes beyond language – it fosters real-world skills that learners can use in their careers, hobbies, and global interactions (Lee & Drajati, 2019a; Rezai et al., 2024a). For example, someone who learns English by gaming might later apply those same communication skills in a virtual work environment or when traveling abroad. In contrast, formal English education provides a structured foundation. Classroom learning focuses on textbooks, grammar drills, and teacher-led lessons to build a strong understanding of grammar, vocabulary, and pronunciation. This approach ensures students develop basic language skills systematically (Dressman et al., 2023). However, in exam-driven systems, the emphasis on achieving correctness and high scores could limit creativity and induce anxiety (Lee, 2020a). For example, students might memorize grammar rules for a test but struggle to use them naturally in conversations.

Formal education often lays a solid groundwork for language learning, offering structure and clarity (Dressman & Sadler, 2020). Yet, in the updated L2 English learning pyramid, Sundqvist (2024) proposes that Extramural English – language exposure beyond the classroom – has become a key individual difference factor, and for many learners, it now serves as the true starting point for acquiring English. This shift aligns somehow with the IDLE Continuum Model, where IDLE complements the limitations of formal instruction by fostering confidence, fluency, and real-world communication skills (Lee, 2022a; Liu et al., 2024). Together, formal education and IDLE form a balanced and dynamic learning ecosystem. A student might master grammar rules in class, then apply them organically by posting on social media, chatting with international teammates in online games, or discussing novels in a virtual book club (Lee, 2022a; Lee et al., 2025). This fusion of structured learning and spontaneous exploration allows learners to build both academic precision and practical fluency – equipping them not only for classroom success but also for meaningful interaction in global, everyday contexts (Sauro & Zourou, 2019).

2.4 The Growth of IDLE Research

The past decade has witnessed an explosive surge in IDLE scholarship, marked by empirical studies, seminal books, and systematic reviews that have shaped the field. Sockett (2014) pioneered work *Online Informal Learning of English*, which mapped how French learners absorbed English organically through digital media like podcasts and web forums. This foundational study redefined perceptions of informal learning, proving its legitimacy as a research-worthy phenomenon.

Meanwhile, Sundqvist (2009, 2019, 2024) carved a parallel path in Northern Europe with their concept of *Extramural English* (also see Sundqvist & Sylvén, 2016). By analyzing Swedish gamers who mastered English through *World of Warcraft* raids and online forums, they revealed how leisure activities could rival – or even surpass – classroom instruction in building fluency. Their work challenged educators to rethink the boundaries between "play" and "learning," urging schools to harness students' digital passions.

The field gained global momentum with Dressman and Sadler's *Handbook of Informal Language Learning* (2020). This volume wove together historical roots, cultural contexts, and case studies from Asia to the Americas, showcasing IDLE's universality. Crucially, it proposed frameworks to bridge informal digital practices with formal curricula – for example, suggesting teachers assign *TikTok* video analyses as homework to validate students' out-of-class learning.

Reinders, Lai, and Sundqvist's *Language Learning Beyond the Classroom* (2022) deepened these insights, offering educators a toolkit of theories, methods, and strategies. The book also demonstrated how to track learners' informal language learning habits to inform lesson plans or use social media analytics to measure linguistic growth, blending rigor with innovation.

Dressman, Lee, and Perrett (2023) then shifted gears from theory to action. Their work delivered ready-to-use lesson plans, such as having students design social media campaigns to practice writing or analyze movie dialogue to study informal language expressions. These strategies showed teachers how to weave IDLE's spontaneity into structured classrooms without sacrificing academic goals.

Most recently, Lee, Zou, and Gu (2024) have propelled the field forward with a teacher-centric guide. Their edited volume equips educators to craft IDLE-aligned activities – like guiding gamers to write strategy guides in English. By prioritizing student interests, these approaches turn hobbies into learning engines, proving that engagement and rigor need not clash.

Review Papers on IDLE

As IDLE research grew, scholars published several review papers. Zhang et al. (2021) analyzed extramural language learning, highlighting that most activities – such as watching videos, listening to music, and reading blogs – were primarily receptive. Their findings emphasized the positive impact of these activities on both linguistic skills (e.g., vocabulary growth) and psychological factors (e.g., motivation and confidence). Soyoof et al. (2023) conducted a scoping review of IDLE, examining its linguistic, cultural, affective, and digital literacy dimensions across Asian and European contexts from 1980 to 2020. They demonstrated how IDLE promotes language learning in a variety of cultural and technological environments.

Lee (2022b) reviewed seventy-six studies on "language learning and teaching beyond the classroom," identifying key gaps in the field, including the need for more rigorous methodologies and innovative tools to assess IDLE's potential. In a related book, Lee (2022a) synthesized findings from multiple studies, showing strong links between IDLE activities and positive outcomes for EFL learners, such as enhanced fluency, motivation, and digital literacy.

Guo and Lee (2023) applied Bronfenbrenner's ecological systems theory (1976, 1979) to explore the factors influencing learners' IDLE engagement. They found that most critical factors operated at the individual and micro-system levels, such as personal interests, peer interactions, and access to technology. They also called for more research on less-studied levels, such as the meso-system (e.g., school–family relationships), exo-system (e.g., societal influences), macro-system (e.g., cultural norms), and chrono-system (e.g., the effects of technological advancements over time). Inspired by Bronfenbrenner's ecological systems theory (1976, 1979), Rezai et al. (2024b) examined teachers' perspectives on students' IDLE engagement, offering strategies to better support learners outside the classroom.

Guan and colleagues (2024) made a significant contribution to IDLE research with a meta-analysis on AI-driven IDLE. Their study revealed that AI tools – such as language-learning chatbots, adaptive apps, and virtual reality platforms – greatly improved learners' English proficiency, self-regulation, and engagement.

Kusyk et al. (2025) carried out a scoping review exploring trends in informal second language learning, analyzing 206 studies published between 2000 and 2020. Their review highlighted a surge in research beginning in 2011, with peak activity between 2017 and 2019. The three most commonly explored themes were second language development (18.2%), mapping informal learning practices (17.5%), and describing informal learning activities (14.3%). They also uncovered a confusing mix of overlapping terms – such as out-of-class language learning, informal second language learning, Extramural English, online informal English learning, and IDLE – leading to what is known as the "jingle-jangle fallacy." The "jingle–jangle fallacy" occurs when different constructs are mistakenly considered the same because they have the same name (*jingle*), or when similar constructs are mistakenly considered different because they have different names (*jangle*; Kelley, 1927). In language learning research, this fallacy can result in conceptual confusion and hinder the comparison of findings across studies (Kusyk et al., 2025). A wide range of theoretical frameworks were applied, including sociocultural theory, complex dynamic systems, learner autonomy, and ecological approaches. Quantitative methods dominated (41%), followed by qualitative (33%) and mixed methods (20%), with surveys (35.7%) and interviews (23%) being the most used tools. The research primarily focused on young adults aged 18–25 (54.4%) and adolescents aged 11–17 (21.8%), with recent studies concentrating on Europe and East Asia. English was the target language in most cases (66.4%). Various learner-related variables were examined, such as usage frequency, attitudes, motivation, activity diversity, confidence in using the second language, and willingness to communicate. Although the review concluded before the rise of AI tools, it offers a comprehensive snapshot of the field's evolution and pinpoints promising directions for future inquiry.

Liu, Soyoof, Lee, and Zhang (2025) conducted a thematic review of IDLE research, analyzing forty-nine empirical studies from Asian EFL contexts published between 2014 and 2024. Echoing the trends identified by Kusyk et al. (2025), they found that IDLE has gained substantial attention, especially in the past four years. Their review revealed that IDLE has been examined through various lenses of individual differences – linguistic, emotional, and cultural. Another key insight was the nuanced and sometimes complicated relationship between teachers and IDLE practices. The study also emphasized how unequal access to digital tools and differing levels of digital literacy shaped learners' participation in IDLE. Drawing from these emerging patterns, the authors proposed several avenues for future research.

Dressman et al. (2025) examined forty-seven narratives drawn from fourteen studies focused on informal language learning. These narratives, rich in ethnographic detail, traced how individuals' language abilities evolved over time in informal settings. By analyzing these stories, the researchers were able to map out seven distinct pathways of language development, shedding light on key factors and circumstances that shape each learner's experience. Their review makes it clear that IDLE does not follow a single, predictable route; instead, it is a highly individualized process shaped by a range of personal and contextual variables.

Emerging Trends and Expanding Horizons

The field of IDLE is witnessing rapid expansion, sparking a proliferation of research that is reshaping our perspectives on language learning in the digital era. For instance, Rezai (2024) and Rezai et al. (2024a) investigated how IDLE influences the professional engagement of EFL teachers. Moving beyond simple observation, they designed a robust instrument to systematically measure teachers' own involvement in digital informal learning. This innovative scale provides concrete metrics for evaluating educators' interactions with digital environments, offering valuable insights into the ways these platforms impact teaching practices.

Meanwhile, the infusion of artificial intelligence into IDLE has become a major focal point. Studies by Guan, Zhang, and Gu (2024), along with Liu, Darvin, and Ma (2024a, 2024b), have uncovered how AI-driven tools are revolutionizing language learning. Innovative technologies such as chatbots simulate real-life conversations, AI-powered writing assistants provide personalized feedback, and immersive virtual reality platforms create engaging environments for practice (Naghdipour, 2022). These tools offer learners tailored, interactive experiences that make practicing English more accessible and enjoyable than ever before.

But the enthusiasm is not confined to English alone. Reflecting our increasingly interconnected world, researchers have begun turning their attention to Languages Other Than English (LOTE). For example, Liu, Zhao, and Yang (2024) explored how learners are informally studying French and German through digital platforms. Using language apps, online communities, and digital media, learners are finding creative and dynamic ways to immerse themselves in new languages. Similarly,

Lee et al. (2023) examined how multilingual learners are picking up Korean through informal digital means. From diving into Korean drama fan sites to joining German gaming forums, these platforms offer authentic, real-world contexts that foster language exposure and practice. Such informal engagement not only increases learners' time spent with the language but also boosts their willingness to communicate and may enhance their overall communicative competence.

3 Antecedents and Consequences of IDLE

As IDLE gains recognition as one of the key subfields within CALL research, scholars have increasingly turned their attention to two main questions (Soyoof et al., 2023; Lee, 2024): How does IDLE influence outcomes? And what motivates individuals to engage in it more frequently?

To date, researchers have identified over forty distinct factors – both causes and effects – linked to IDLE. These findings, illustrated in Figure 3, offer rich insights into how IDLE shapes the learning journey and what encourages individuals to participate. For example, those who engage in receptive activities (e.g., watching English YouTube videos) or productive ones (e.g., chatting with English speakers) often report a wide range of benefits. These include emotional gains (e.g., increased enjoyment), psychological boosts (e.g., enhanced psychological well-being), academic

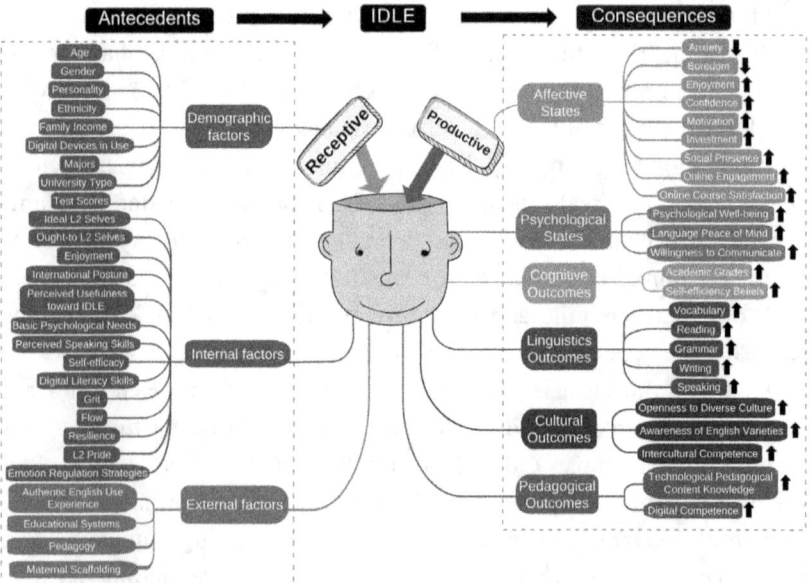

Figure 3 Antecedents and Consequences of IDLE

improvements (e.g., better grades), linguistic development (e.g., vocabulary growth), cultural awareness (e.g., becoming more tolerant toward varieties of English), and even digital literacy.

On the flip side, several factors have been found to influence IDLE participation. These include demographic traits (e.g., age), internal characteristics (e.g., international outlook), and external conditions (e.g., the structure of the education system). Mapping these relationships provides a valuable evidence base for educators and researchers to design, adapt, and implement IDLE activities or intervention programs in ways that are both scientifically grounded and locally relevant (Lee et al., 2025).

3.1 Consequences of IDLE

This section explores the wide-ranging benefits of IDLE, focusing on six major areas: emotional, psychological, cognitive, linguistic, cultural, and pedagogical. The first five notably influence learners, while the pedagogical impact is most relevant to educators. Growing research suggests that IDLE holds the potential to reshape how students learn new languages and how teachers design their lessons. Each domain below presents key research findings and the scholars behind them, followed by a discussion of these results. Since most evidence is correlational, it is important to interpret these findings with appropriate caution.

Affective Benefits

- Lowered anxiety (Lee & Xie, 2023; Uztosun & Kök, 2023; Wouters et al., 2024; Rezai et al., 2025)
- Less boredom (Taherian et al., 2023)
- Greater enjoyment (Lai et al., 2015; Lee & Lee, 2021; Lee & Xie, 2023; Tsang & Lee, 2023; Lee et al., 2024; Liu et al., 2024; Fu, 2025; Rezai et al., 2025)
- Increased confidence (Lai et al., 2015; Lee & Drajati, 2019b; Zou et al., 2025)
- Heightened motivation (Lee & Drajati, 2019b; Tsang & Lee, 2023; Wouters et al., 2024; Rezai et al., 2025)
- Stronger investment (Liu & Darvin, 2023)
- Enhanced social presence (Wu, 2023)
- Higher online engagement (Wu, 2023)
- Higher online course satisfaction (Zheng & Xiao, 2024)

Learning and teaching a new language are deeply emotional processes (Richards, 2020). For teachers, understanding and responding to learners' emotions is a core professional skill. For students, emotions shape how they approach and absorb new knowledge. In recent years, the field has experienced an "affective turn" (Prior, 2019), as researchers increasingly acknowledge the central role of emotions in language learning. Early studies focused mostly on negative emotions – anxiety, fear, or shame – but the rise of positive psychology has ushered in a wave of research on positive experiences in language acquisition (Dewaele & MacIntyre, 2014, 2016). Positive psychology seeks not just fleeting happiness but authentic well-being, resilience, fulfillment, and a sense of being true to oneself (MacIntyre et al., 2016). This has shifted scholarly attention toward the power of positive emotions to enhance language learning.

This new focus on emotion and well-being has deeply influenced research on IDLE. Studies now suggest that IDLE significantly shapes learners' emotions and attitudes, nurturing positive feelings while easing negative ones (Lai et al., 2015; Lee & Lee, 2021; Uztosun & Kök, 2023). IDLE reduces the anxiety common in language learning by creating a relaxed, low-pressure environment. Digital tools (e.g., language apps and educational games) let students practice English at their own rhythm, free from the scrutiny and stress of the traditional classroom. This sense of autonomy makes learners more comfortable and less afraid of making linguistic mistakes (Uztosun & Kök, 2023; Wouters et al., 2024).

Lee and Xie (2023), using a person-centered approach, found intriguing patterns among 1,265 Korean EFL learners who participated in a variety of IDLE activities. Their findings showed that students who balanced their IDLE time across gaming, entertainment, English learning, and social interaction experienced noticeably less anxiety during face-to-face English conversations than those whose IDLE activities revolved mainly around gaming and entertainment.

But the benefits of IDLE go beyond reducing anxiety – it also injects excitement and genuine interest into language learning (Lee & Lee, 2021; Liu et al., 2024). Interactive digital platforms turn what could be a monotonous task into an engaging, playful journey, sparking curiosity and making learning feel meaningful and fun (Taherian et al., 2023). Lee and Xie (2023) further discovered that learners who diversified their IDLE experiences – incorporating English learning and socialization along with entertainment – reported greater enjoyment in studying English than those who stuck only to gaming and entertainment. The hands-on, interactive features of these digital tools keep learners actively involved, boosting both their motivation and enthusiasm.

Learners often discover real enjoyment in self-directed activities tailored to their own interests (Liu et al., 2024; Rezai et al., 2025). Whether it is watching English-language YouTube videos, joining online communities, or exploring digital content tied to their hobbies, these experiences allow students to connect with English in ways that feel meaningful and fun (Lai et al., 2015; Lee & Lee, 2021). Here, learning blends seamlessly with leisure, making progress feel less like work and more like play (Chik & Ho, 2017).

Small wins – such as understanding a movie without subtitles or confidently posting in an online forum – can give learners a powerful boost in self-belief (Zadorozhnyy & Lee, 2023). Each success story strengthens their confidence and encourages them to keep going (Lai et al., 2015; Lee & Drajati, 2019b). This growing self-assurance motivates learners to take on new challenges and fosters a positive image of themselves as capable language users (Lee & Lee, 2021; Liu & Lee, 2023; Liu et al., 2024; Fu, 2025).

IDLE naturally integrates language practice into learners' daily passions, whether that is gaming, music, or social media (Dressman et al., 2023). When learning is woven into activities they already love, motivation and commitment soar (Lee & Lee, 2021; Guan et al., 2024). This relevance inspires learners to invest more time and energy, making English a natural and enjoyable part of everyday life (Liu et al., 2023).

Digital platforms also build a strong sense of community, connecting learners with peers around the world (Sauro, 2017; Vazquez-Calvo et al., 2019). Through online discussions, comments, and collaboration, students gain a sense of belonging to a supportive network where they can share, learn, and encourage each other (Wu, 2023). Such connections not only increase motivation but also provide the emotional support needed for sustained learning (Zadorozhnyy & Lee, 2025).

Zheng and Xiao (2024) explored how engaging in IDLE influences online course satisfaction among 563 Chinese university EFL students. Their findings revealed that students who participated in IDLE activities more often felt more satisfied with their online courses, appreciating both the course design and their teachers' effectiveness. The study also uncovered that self-regulated learning online played a key mediating role in this relationship. In other words, students who frequently engaged in IDLE tended to develop stronger self-regulation skills, such as setting goals, managing their time, using effective learning strategies, and evaluating their own progress. These enhanced skills, in turn, boosted their satisfaction with online courses.

Psychological Benefits

- Better psychological well-being (Lee & Chiu, 2024)
- Greater autonomy and sense of relatedness (Wu & Wang, 2025)
- Growth in self-regulated online learning (Rezai & Goodarzi, 2025)
- Flow experiences (Wu & Wang, 2025)
- Increased grit (Lee & Lu, 2023; Liu & Lee, 2023; Fu, 2025)
- Greater peace of mind in language learning (Ghasemi & Noughabi, 2024)
- Higher willingness to communicate (Lee & Drajati, 2019b; Taherian et al., 2023; Zadorozhnyy & Lee, 2023; Lee & Chiu, 2024; Liu et al., 2024; Yang et al., 2024; Fu, 2025; Guo et al., 2025; Lee et al., 2025)

The psychological rewards of engaging in IDLE reach well beyond simple language gains – they play a powerful role in nurturing learners' mental health and boosting their openness to communication (Taherian et al., 2023; Lee & Chiu, 2024; Yang et al., 2024). By creating a low-stress, supportive learning space, IDLE helps foster a sense of balance and well-being in daily life (Lee & Chiu, 2024). When students interact with enjoyable digital platforms, language study becomes not just more relaxed, but also more personally satisfying compared to traditional classroom approaches (Liu & Lee, 2023; Ghasemi & Noughabi, 2024). For instance, Rezai and Goodarzi (2025) discovered that among 325 Iranian EFL students, those who used IDLE more frequently displayed stronger skills in self-regulated online learning. These learners excelled at setting goals, organizing their study environment, developing effective strategies, managing their time, seeking help when needed, and evaluating their own progress.

Wu and Wang (2025) discovered that when 333 Chinese university students used GenAI-supported IDLE, they often entered a state of "flow" – that deep, effortless concentration where learning feels both easy and enjoyable (Csikszentmihalyi, 2014). Importantly, these students also felt a greater sense of independence and a stronger bond with others – two key factors for psychological well-being. This shows that GenAI-powered language activities can help students take charge of their own learning while feeling connected, even in a digital environment.

IDLE also nurtures "grit" – the determination to keep trying and stay interested, even when faced with setbacks (Duckworth, 2017). By giving learners the chance to repeatedly face new challenges and still enjoy the process, IDLE has the potential for strengthening their grit (Liu & Lee, 2023; Fu, 2025). Lee and Xie (2023), using a person-centered approach, found that Korean EFL learners who balanced their IDLE time among gaming, entertainment, English study, and socializing showed much more grit than those who focused mainly on gaming and entertainment.

Another key psychological benefit is what researchers describe as "foreign language peace of mind" – a comforting sense of inner calm and coherence while navigating a new language (Ghasemi & Noughabi, 2024). Among 316 Iranian EFL students, those who regularly engaged in IDLE activities – whether listening, reading, writing, or speaking – reported feeling more at ease with English, which in turn boosted their willingness to communicate. Free from the anxiety of being judged or making mistakes, learners can experiment, participate in online conversations, comment on social media, or use language apps without the fear that often shadows classroom settings. This growing sense of ease naturally leads to greater willingness to communicate, even in unfamiliar or real-world situations. As learners become more confident and adept, they are more likely to start conversations, offer opinions, or connect with strangers – actions they might have shied away from before (Ghasemi & Noughabi, 2024; Lee et al., 2024).

Cognitive Advantages

- Improved academic achievement (Lai et al., 2015; Sundqvist & Wikström, 2015)
- Stronger performance on standardized English exams (Zou et al., 2025)
- Greater self-efficacy (Zadorozhnyy & Lee, 2023)

IDLE does not just broaden learners' language skills – it fuels cognitive growth on multiple levels. When students immerse themselves in informal digital activities – like exploring educational apps, watching insightful videos, or joining online discussions – they add meaningful layers to their formal education. Research by Lai et al. (2015) and Sundqvist and Wikström (2015) shows that this combination of formal and informal learning often leads to higher grades and better classroom participation. Supporting this, Zou et al. (2025) found that Chinese university students who regularly participated in meaning-focused IDLE activities scored higher on the College English Test Band 4 (CET-4), a rigorous, nationwide exam that measures listening, reading, writing, and translation skills across China. The CET-4, much like academic grades, is designed to assess a wide range of cognitive abilities, from comprehension to language production. In this way, IDLE acts as both a language booster and a cognitive catalyst – helping students achieve more in their studies while strengthening their ability to analyze, understand, and use English in practical contexts.

Beyond academic results, IDLE fosters a stronger sense of self-efficacy – the conviction that one can take charge of their own learning process (Zadorozhnyy & Lee, 2023). When students make choices about what and how to learn, they gain confidence and stay motivated, consistently building their language skills. Zadorozhnyy and Lee (2023) highlight how this sense of ownership leads to steady progress and personal development.

Linguistic Benefits

- Expanded vocabulary (Sundqvist & Wikström, 2015; Jensen, 2017; Sundqvist, 2019; Alhaq, 2022; Lai et al., 2022; Warnby, 2022; Lai & Wang, 2024, 2025; Rezai et al., 2024c)
- Sharper reading comprehension (Cole & Vanderplank, 2016; Rezai et al., 2025)
- Deeper understanding of grammar (Cole & Vanderplank, 2016)
- Stronger writing skills (Kusyk, 2017)
- Enhanced speaking abilities (Sundqvist, 2009; Lee & Dressman, 2018; Tsang & Lee, 2023)

One of IDLE's greatest advantages is its ability to boost every aspect of language proficiency. When learners immerse themselves in genuine, everyday situations – such as gaming online, watching streaming videos, or chatting on social media – they naturally pick up fresh vocabulary, including slang and expressions rarely found in traditional textbooks (De Wilde et al., 2022; Lai & Wang, 2024). This natural exposure leads to a richer, more practical command of language (Sundqvist, 2009; Lee & Dressman, 2018). Watching movies or TV with subtitles, browsing blogs, and reading online articles all sharpen reading comprehension skills (Cole & Vanderplank, 2016; Rezai et al., 2025). For example, Rezai et al. (2025) found that Iranian university students who participated in both extra-curricular and informal IDLE activities showed significantly higher reading comprehension scores than those in the control group.

Engaging with a wide range of written texts allows learners to decode meanings, appreciate different writing styles, and handle increasingly complex content (Cole & Vanderplank, 2016; Tsang, 2023). Frequent encounters with natural language in context mean learners start to pick up grammar intuitively, without needing to memorize endless rules (Cole & Vanderplank, 2016). Observing and hearing correct usage in everyday settings helps them internalize grammatical structures, making their language use more accurate and fluid (Arndt & Woore, 2018).

Writing skills also get a boost as students engage in real communication – whether it is posting on forums, leaving comments, or keeping online journals (Kusyk, 2017). These activities sharpen their ability to organize thoughts, express ideas clearly, and tailor their writing for different audiences. Meanwhile, video chats, multiplayer games, and interactive online discussions offer a safe space to practice speaking, improving both fluency and pronunciation by mimicking native speakers and interacting in real time (Lee & Dressman, 2018; Tsang & Lee, 2023). By combining a range of IDLE activities with targeted classroom support from teachers to address anything not picked up through IDLE, IDLE fosters the development of well-rounded language skills (Schurz & Sundqvist, 2022).

Cultural Awareness

- Openness to diverse cultures (Liu et al., 2023)
- Awareness of English varieties (Lee & Drajati, 2019a; Lee, 2020b; Lee et al., 2024)
- Development of intercultural competence (Lee, 2020b; Liu et al., 2023)

IDLE does far more than build language skills – it serves as a powerful gateway to cultural awareness, immersing learners in a tapestry of perspectives and ideas from around the globe (Lee, 2020b; Liu et al., 2023; Lee et al., 2024). When learners dive into international content, they are not simply acquiring new vocabulary or grammar; they are stepping into new worlds, encountering different traditions, beliefs, and viewpoints that expand their understanding of what it means to be part of a global society (Liu et al., 2023).

Engaging with authentic materials – whether it is watching foreign films, reading international literature, or joining global online discussions – pushes learners to open their minds and adapt to unfamiliar cultural experiences (Liu et al., 2023). This kind of exposure not only nurtures curiosity and appreciation for diversity, but it also breaks down stereotypes, fostering empathy and genuine respect for others (Liu et al., 2023). As learners connect with realities beyond their own, they become more inclusive and better equipped to navigate an interconnected world (Lee, 2022a).

Through IDLE, learners encounter a rich array of English accents and dialects, deepening their appreciation for the language's diversity on a global scale (Lee & Drajati, 2019a; Lee, 2020b). Hearing English spoken in countless varieties – from British and American to Australian, Indian, or Korean – highlights its role as a living, evolving lingua franca (Graddol, 2006; Crystal, 2010). This awareness encourages learners to become flexible communicators, comfortable with the many ways English is shaped by different cultures and histories (Lee & Drajati, 2019a).

Such wide-ranging exposure naturally builds intercultural competence, arming learners with the confidence and sensitivity needed for effective cross-cultural communication (Lee & Drajati, 2019a). They become skilled at interpreting subtle cultural cues and adjusting their communication styles to bridge differences. True intercultural competence means moving beyond awareness – it is about applying empathy, active listening, and adaptability in real-life interactions across diverse settings. By nurturing cultural awareness, IDLE prepares learners to actively participate in our interconnected world (Lee, 2020b; Liu et al., 2023). It empowers them to engage in thoughtful conversations, work collaboratively with people from all backgrounds, and make meaningful contributions to global communities. In this way, IDLE not only advances cultural fluency – an invaluable asset in today's multicultural societies and workplaces – but also supports the lifelong learning journey envisioned by the UN SDGs, ensuring learners are prepared to contribute meaningfully throughout their lives (Sundqvist, 2022).

Pedagogical Enhancements

- Stronger technological pedagogical content knowledge (Rezai et al., 2024a)
- Greater digital competence (Rezai et al., 2024a)
- Job engagement (Rezai et al., 2024a)

The impact of IDLE is not limited to students – it powerfully empowers educators as well, allowing them to elevate their teaching and seamlessly weave technology into their classrooms. For example, Rezai et al. (2024a) explored how IDLE relates to technological pedagogical content knowledge (TPACK), digital competence, and job engagement among 375 Iranian EFL teachers. Their findings revealed a strong positive connection: teachers who engaged with IDLE displayed higher levels of TPACK and digital competence, which in turn boosted their engagement and enthusiasm for their work. Notably, both TPACK and digital competence served as bridges, linking IDLE involvement to increased job satisfaction and commitment. These results highlight that IDLE not only advances teachers' technological and pedagogical skills but also fuels their passion for teaching, fostering a more dynamic, innovative, and rewarding classroom environment.

However, it is important to recognize that not every teacher is able to enhance their pedagogical or technological skills. For example, Becker (2022) found that most of the seventy-three EFL teachers surveyed in North Rhine-Westphalia, Germany, had never used video games in their teaching. Many cited a lack of interest in video games, uncertainty about effective methods, and unfamiliarity with the necessary teaching strategies. Similar barriers were reported by Hong Kong EFL teachers in Zadorozhnyy et al. (2025). Based on 470 survey responses from 159 teachers collected between 2019 and 2024, the challenges to integrating IDLE stemmed from both internal factors (like insufficient training and familiarity) and external pressures (such as exam-driven curricula and heavy workloads). Therefore, it becomes clear that while individual initiative is important, broader systemic or structural support is also essential to help teachers successfully bring innovative pedagogies like IDLE into schools.

3.2 Antecedents of IDLE

The exploration of IDLE's benefits has sparked a deep interest in understanding the factors that encourage and sustain learners' engagement with these digital learning environments. Researchers are eager to uncover what drives individuals to adopt IDLE practices and how these motivators can be nurtured to enhance language learning outcomes. These influential factors are grouped into three main categories: sociobiographic, learner-internal, and learner-external.

Sociobiographic Factors

- Gender (Zhang & Liu, 2023)
- Age (Rezai et al., 2024b)
- Personality traits (Rezai et al., 2024b)
- Family income (Rezai et al., 2024b)
- Ethnicity (Zhang & Liu, 2023; Rezai et al., 2024b)
- Number of digital devices in use (Zhang & Liu, 2023)
- Majors (Zhang & Liu, 2023)
- University type (Zhang & Liu, 2023)
- Standardized test results (Zhang & Liu, 2023)

The demographic and social characteristics of learners significantly influence how they engage with IDLE. Elements, such as gender, age, personality traits, socioeconomic status, cultural background, ethnicity, and academic background, all play crucial roles in shaping their participation.

Gender impacts engagement levels in notable ways (Zhang & Liu, 2023). Research indicates that males and females often differ not only in how frequently they interact with IDLE but also in the types of activities they prefer (Zhang & Liu, 2023). For example, male learners might be more drawn to competitive gaming platforms or technology-focused forums, while female learners may gravitate toward collaborative learning apps or social media communities that foster communication and connection.

Age is another important factor influencing engagement with IDLE (Rezai et al., 2024b). Younger learners tend to favor games and entertainment-based methods, finding interactive apps, virtual reality experiences, and gamified learning platforms both engaging and relatable (Butler, 2015; Sundqvist & Wikström, 2015). These tools align with their familiarity with digital entertainment and their desire for immersive experiences. By contrast, older learners often prefer structured or academic content, such as online courses, webinars, and educational websites that provide formal instruction with clear objectives and outcomes (Rezai et al., 2024b). They might appreciate organized content that mirrors traditional educational settings and offers depth in specific subject areas.

Personality traits profoundly shape how learners approach IDLE (Rezai et al., 2024b). Individuals who are open to new experiences may eagerly explore diverse digital resources, experiment with unconventional learning methods, and embrace cutting-edge technologies. Their curiosity drives them to seek out innovative platforms and engage with a variety of content. On the other hand, learners who exhibit conscientiousness might adopt disciplined study schedules, utilize organized apps with progress-tracking features, and prefer platforms that allow them to set goals and monitor achievements (Rezai et al., 2024b). Their methodical nature ensures they make consistent progress and maintain focus on their learning objectives.

Socioeconomic status can greatly shape a learner's experience with IDLE (Rezai et al., 2024b). Family income, for instance, often determines whether students have easy access to essential technology such as computers, tablets, or stable internet (Rezai et al., 2024b). Students from wealthier households typically enjoy a range of digital devices at their fingertips, allowing them to explore online resources freely and without barriers. In contrast, those from less advantaged backgrounds may struggle with limited or shared devices and unreliable internet, making it harder to fully participate in independent digital learning (Zhang & Liu, 2023). This gap reflects broader issues of digital inequality, where access, adaptability, and the ability to create knowledge using technology are crucial for inclusion in today's digital world (Warschauer, 2003). However, our research also shows that simply having access to devices and resources – which is often the case for students from higher socioeconomic backgrounds – does not automatically guarantee effective learning (Lee, 2019). What truly matters is how students use these tools to achieve meaningful outcomes. Warschauer (2003) highlighted this point by critiquing the "hole-in-the-wall" project in India, where merely installing computer kiosks in communities did not necessarily lead to positive learning experiences, and sometimes even proved harmful. As he aptly put it, "minimally invasive education was, in practice, minimally effective education" (Warschauer, 2003, p. 2). This underscores the importance of thoughtfully guided use of technology, rather than relying solely on access.

Cultural background and ethnicity significantly influence learners' attitudes toward IDLE (Zhang & Liu, 2023; Rezai et al., 2024b). Cultural values and societal norms affect how learners perceive digital learning and the importance they place on acquiring English through digital means. For instance, in some cultures, there may be a strong emphasis on traditional face-to-face instruction, valuing direct interaction with teachers and classmates. In others, there might be widespread encouragement to embrace technology in education, viewing digital tools as essential for advancement and global communication. These cultural differences shape learners' preferences, the types of content they engage with, and how much value they assign to digital English learning (Zhang & Liu, 2023; Rezai et al., 2024b). Understanding these nuances is crucial for developing effective and culturally responsive educational strategies.

Academic background is another key factor impacting engagement with IDLE (Zhang & Liu, 2023). A learner's field of study, the type of university or educational institution they attend, and their academic performance can influence their participation. Students majoring in English, linguistics, or related disciplines may engage more actively in IDLE because it directly supports their academic and career aspirations (Zhang & Liu, 2023). For example, a student studying international relations might use language exchange apps to practice English with peers worldwide, enhancing both their language skills and cultural understanding. Similarly, learners with higher test scores or those attending universities that prioritize technology integration may be more inclined to incorporate IDLE into their learning routines (Zhang & Liu, 2023). Their academic environment fosters an atmosphere where digital learning is encouraged and readily accessible.

Internal Factors

- Ideal L2 selves (Lee & Lu, 2023; Liu et al., 2023, 2024b; Zou et al., 2025)
- Ought-to L2 selves (Liu et al., 2024b; Zou et al., 2025)
- Enjoyment (Liu et al., 2024b)
- International posture (Liu et al., 2023)
- Perceived usefulness toward IDLE (Zhang & Liu, 2022; Lee & Chiu, 2023; Liu et al., 2024; Rezai et al., 2024b)
- Basic psychological needs (Fathali & Okada, 2018; Sockett & Toffoli, 2020; Toffoli, 2020; Jeon, 2022; Zadorozhnyy & Lee, 2024, 2025)
- Perceived speaking skills (Zhang & Liu, 2023)
- Self-efficacy (Barkati et al., 2024)
- Digital literacy skills (Barkati et al., 2024; Rezai et al., 2024b)
- Grit (Barkati et al., 2024)
- Pride (Zou et al., 2025)
- Emotion regulation strategies (Guo et al., 2025)

Learner-internal factors revolve around the personal characteristics and psychological traits that drive individuals to participate in IDLE. These internal motivations are deeply rooted in how learners perceive themselves and their aspirations in mastering the English language.

One key driving force is the idea of the learner's "ideal L2 self" – the vision they hold of themselves as confident, capable English speakers in the future (Dörnyei, 2009). This imagined self becomes a powerful source of motivation, pushing learners to immerse themselves in IDLE as they work toward making this vision a reality (Lee & Lu, 2023; Liu et al., 2023; Liu et al., 2024b; Zou et al., 2025). For example, Lee and Lu (2023) interviewed a student named Tim, who shared, "I have a few foreign friends on WeChat [Chinese popular social media]. We have become friends during the overseas music contest. I often talk about the music and musical instruments to them on WeChat [through speaking and typing] in my spare time" (p. 137). Tim's experience highlights how a vivid ideal L2 self can encourage Chinese EFL students to actively participate in IDLE activities.

Alongside this internal motivation is the notion of the "ought-to L2 self," which captures the external expectations and pressures learners feel – from academic demands, career ambitions, or broader cultural values that stress the importance of English (Dörnyei, 2009). These outside influences create a sense of duty, further fueling learners' commitment to mastering the language (Liu et al., 2023; Liu et al., 2024b; Zou et al., 2025). These dual motivations – the ideal and ought-to selves – combine to push learners to actively seek out and persist in IDLE activities. The desire to fulfill personal aspirations while meeting societal expectations creates a strong internal drive that sustains their engagement over time.

Enjoyment plays a vital role in shaping learners' dedication to IDLE (Liu et al., 2024b). When students truly find joy and satisfaction in their digital language activities, they are much more likely to stick with them (Liu et al., 2024b). This sense of enjoyment often springs from interactive language games, dynamic multimedia content, or meaningful online exchanges with others (Lee, 2022a). Such positive experiences not only boost motivation but also transform language learning into a fun, engaging pursuit rather than a tedious obligation (Papi & Hiver, 2025).

While Lin (2023) did not directly measure enjoyment, the study focused on L2 interest – closely related to pleasure in learning – among 631 university students in the US taking various language courses (Chinese, French, Russian, and Spanish). Using "out-of-class L2 contact" as a variable, Lin tracked how often students used language resources outside the classroom, such as social media, movies, music, news, and emails. The findings revealed that students with higher interest in their new language engaged more frequently with these digital resources, suggesting that genuine curiosity and enjoyment can drive greater involvement in IDLE.

Another important motivator is the learner's "international posture," which refers to how they see themselves fitting into the global community (Yashima, 2002; Liu et al., 2023). Learners with a strong international posture recognize that English is a global lingua franca and view proficiency in the language as a gateway to connecting with people worldwide. This perspective encourages them to engage with IDLE to enhance their ability to communicate across cultures, participate in international dialogues, and access global opportunities (Dizon, 2023; Lee & Lu, 2023).

Learners' engagement with IDLE is strongly influenced by how beneficial they perceive it to be for achieving their own educational and career ambitions (Zhang & Liu, 2022; Lee & Chiu, 2023; Liu et al., 2024; Rezai et al., 2024b). When students believe that IDLE can help them communicate more effectively, excel academically, or advance professionally, they become more willing to invest their time and effort. This practical recognition of IDLE's value not only strengthens their motivation but also reinforces their commitment. The positive impact of IDLE is not limited to students alone; preservice English teachers benefit as well. Kusuma et al. (2024) found that when EFL preservice teachers had rewarding experiences with IDLE in high school or through interactions with peers, they gained a deeper appreciation for its advantages and developed more positive attitudes toward its use. These encouraging attitudes could inspire future EFL teachers to incorporate IDLE into their own classrooms, potentially creating a lasting ripple effect on the students they teach. However, to fully understand the long-term impact of this process, further empirical research is needed.

The satisfaction of basic psychological needs, as outlined in self-determination theory, is also crucial in motivating learners (Deci & Ryan, 1985). This theory emphasizes three fundamental needs: autonomy, competence, and relatedness (Fathali & Okada, 2018; Sockett & Toffoli, 2020; Toffoli, 2020; Jeon, 2022; Zadorozhnyy & Lee, 2024). Learners who feel autonomous experience a sense of control over their learning choices and paths. Those who feel competent believe in their ability to succeed and master the language. The sense of relatedness refers to feeling connected with others – peers, instructors, or online communities – which can provide support and encouragement. When these needs are met, learners are more intrinsically motivated and actively engaged in IDLE. For example, learners who are confident in their speaking skills and possess strong self-efficacy – the belief in their ability to achieve goals – tend to participate more actively and effectively in digital language learning environments (Bandura, 1997; Barkati et al., 2024). This confidence allows them to tackle challenging tasks, engage in conversations without excessive fear of making mistakes, and persist despite obstacles.

Additional personal traits such as grit, resilience, and the ability to achieve a state of "flow" also play significant roles (Csikszentmihalyi, 2014; Barkati et al., 2024; Gao et al., 2025). Grit involves perseverance and passion for long-term goals, enabling learners to stay committed to language learning even when faced with difficulties (Liu & Lee, 2023). Grit allows them to recover quickly from setbacks, maintaining their motivation and drive (Duckworth, 2017). Achieving a state of flow – a deep immersion and enjoyment in an activity – enhances learning outcomes by fostering intense focus and a sense of fulfillment during IDLE activities (Csikszentmihalyi, 2014; Gao et al., 2025).

Digital literacy is a critical factor influencing learners' engagement with IDLE (Barkati et al., 2024; Rezai et al., 2024b). Learners must possess the necessary skills to navigate digital platforms, utilize online resources, and communicate effectively in virtual environments. Proficiency in using technology enables them to access a wide array of learning materials, participate in online communities, and tailor their learning experiences to their individual needs. Without sufficient digital literacy, learners may struggle to engage fully with IDLE, hindering their ability to benefit from its offerings (Rezai et al., 2024b).

Pride can be seen as a self-aware emotion that arises from achieving something meaningful, rooted in one's own sense of accomplishment (Buechner et al., 2018). It has two main forms: pride in personal achievement and pride from comparing oneself favorably to others. Zou et al. (2025) discovered that feeling proud of one's second language skills is closely connected to greater involvement in IDLE activities. This connection suggests that experiencing L2 pride gives students valuable chances to display their English abilities, which can boost their confidence and inspire them to engage even more in digital English learning beyond the classroom.

Guo et al. (2025) looked at how the ways students manage their emotions – specifically, through cognitive reappraisal and expressive suppression – relate to different styles of IDLE among 829 participants. *Cognitive reappraisal* is when someone tries to think about a situation differently to change how they feel about it – for example, seeing a tough assignment as a learning opportunity rather than a setback. *Expressive suppression*, on the other hand, is when someone tries to hide or hold back their emotional reactions, like keeping a straight face even when frustrated. The study found that students who regularly used *cognitive reappraisal* were much more likely to be in the "Active" group of IDLE learners, meaning they engaged more often and with greater enthusiasm in informal English learning online. In contrast, those who used *expressive suppression* less frequently tended to be "Passive" learners, participating less actively. In short, students who reframe their feelings in a positive way are more engaged in IDLE, while those who bottle up their emotions are more likely to take a backseat in their learning.

External Factors

- Maternal scaffolding (Soyoof et al., 2024)
- Pedagogy (Peng et al., 2025)
- Authentic English use experience (Zhang & Liu, 2022; Lee & Chiu, 2023)
- Educational systems (Rezai et al., 2024b)

External factors encompass the social and environmental conditions that shape how learners participate in IDLE. These elements, existing outside the individual, play a significant role in influencing learners' engagement with informal digital language learning.

Parental support is a significant factor shaping learners' engagement in IDLE activities (Soyoof et al., 2024). When parents actively encourage and assist their children's language learning, they can create meaningful opportunities for practice and growth (Tao & Xu, 2022; Seo, 2025). This support may involve providing technological resources – such as computers, tablets, or smartphones with internet access – and recommending educational websites, language learning apps, or online courses (Seo, 2025). For example, parents might introduce interactive English-learning games or encourage watching educational videos in English. However, it is important to acknowledge that not all parents have the same level of resources or digital literacy, which can affect the consistency and effectiveness of their involvement (Guo & Lee, 2023). Additionally, while parental encouragement can be highly beneficial, excessive pressure or unrealistic expectations may sometimes lead to anxiety or reduced motivation for learners (Park, 2009).

With respect to teacher pedagogy, Peng et al. (2025) carried out a study with seventy Iranian female EFL learners to explore the impact of innovative teaching methods. Over eight weeks, participants attended seventeen sessions of podcast-enhanced speaking classes, each lasting 90 minutes and held twice a week. The podcasts delved into a wide range of topics, from technology and culture to global issues. To encourage learning beyond the classroom, students were also assigned supplementary activities – reviewing podcasts, joining online discussion forums, and keeping reflective journals – to deepen their experience with IDLE. In this study, IDLE was assessed broadly, covering form-focused, game-based, receptive, and productive activities. The results showed that students who participated in the podcast-integrated speaking sessions demonstrated significantly higher engagement in IDLE than those in the control group.

Exposure to authentic English greatly enhances learners' motivation and engagement (Zhang & Liu, 2022; Lee & Chiu, 2023). Interacting with native speakers provides practical experience that helps learners grasp nuances, idioms, and cultural references inherent in everyday communication. This interaction might occur through language exchange programs, online chat platforms, or international social networks (Lee, 2022a). Additionally, consuming real-world English content, such as movies, television shows, music, podcasts, and books, immerses learners in the language in a natural and engaging way. For example, a student who regularly watches English-language films or participates in online communities centered around topics of interest may develop stronger language skills and increased confidence in using English. This authentic exposure makes learning more relevant and enjoyable, reinforcing their commitment to improving their proficiency (Zhang & Liu, 2022; Lee & Chiu, 2023).

Educational institutions, including schools and universities, play a crucial role in either promoting or hindering IDLE participation (Rezai et al., 2024b). When these institutions integrate digital tools into their teaching, they provide students with additional avenues to engage with the language outside traditional classroom settings. For instance, a school might incorporate language learning apps into the curriculum, offer access to online English resources, or encourage the use of educational technology in assignments. Teachers can provide guidance on effective practices, such as how to utilize online forums for language exchange or how to critically evaluate digital content. By creating environments that promote independent learning, educational institutions empower students to take control of their language development and explore resources that align with their interests and learning styles. Conversely, if schools neglect to provide technological access or discourage the use of digital platforms, they may unintentionally block students from benefiting from IDLE opportunities (Rezai et al., 2024b).

In the next section, we will delve into practical ways to embed IDLE into educational systems, exploring concrete steps and initiatives that can ensure its long-term success. This includes discussing policy recommendations, curriculum integration, teacher training, and community involvement to create a holistic approach that benefits learners at all levels.

4 Bringing IDLE into Schools and Communities

4.1 Challenges of Bringing IDLE into Formal Education

For a decade or so, researchers and educators have championed the integration of IDLE into formal education (Lee & Chik, 2025). Yet, its adoption has been slow and uneven (Sundqvist & Sylvén, 2016; Arndt & Lyrigkou, 2019; Hubbard, 2020; Lee, 2022b; Dressman et al., 2023). A variety of obstacles – ranging from systemic limitations to teacher readiness and local educational conditions – stand in the way of widespread implementation (Zadorozhnyy et al., 2025).

Take Hong Kong as an example: structural barriers make up 73% of the challenges to IDLE adoption. Among these, two major issues dominate – overburdened teachers (50%) and rigid, exam-focused curricula (23%; Zadorozhnyy et al., 2024, 2025). These pressures leave little room for experimenting with innovative methods like IDLE, as the emphasis remains on meeting institutional goals.

By contrast, Indonesian schools face a different set of hurdles, with 64.8% of obstacles stemming from individual and local factors. These include gaps in teacher skills (21.3%), difficulties motivating students (22.2%), and infrastructure problems like unreliable Wi-Fi (10.2%; Lee, 2024). These examples illustrate how the challenges of implementing IDLE vary significantly depending on the country's education policies, resources, and classroom dynamics.

Efforts to introduce IDLE often fail when implemented through top-down directives that ignore local realities (Lee et al., 2025; Zadorozhnyy et al., 2025). While national policies may endorse IDLE in theory, its success depends on how well schools and teachers adapt it to their specific circumstances (Lee et al., 2025). Without addressing the unique structural and contextual challenges in each setting, IDLE remains an underused and undervalued teaching approach (see Figure 4).

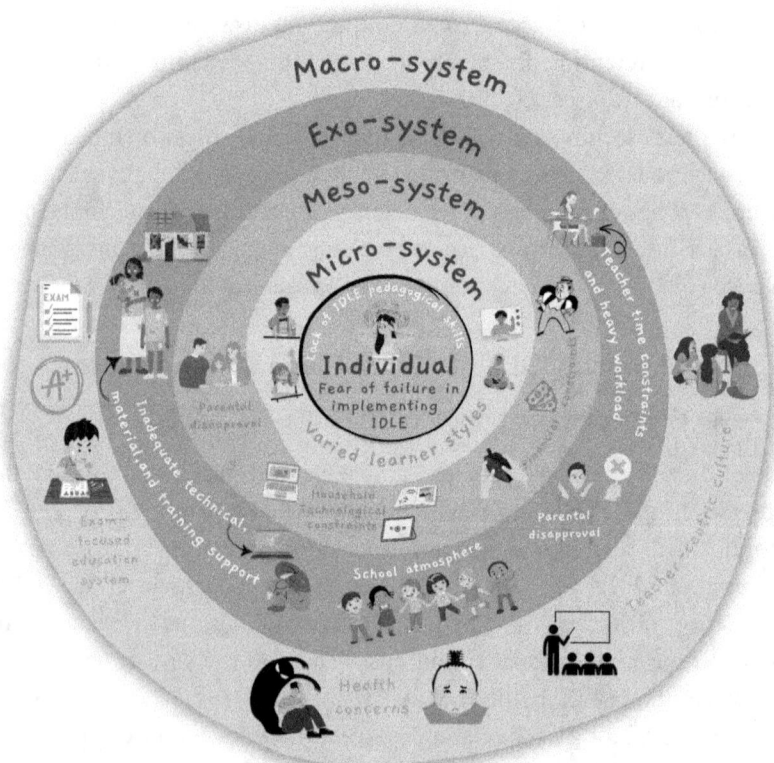

Figure 4 Ecological Factors Affecting Teachers' IDLE Integration into Practice

4.2 The IDLE Continuum Model

The IDLE Continuum Model offers a practical, adaptable framework for blending informal digital learning with formal education (Lee, 2022a). Instead of relying on rigid, top-down methods, this model emphasizes a bottom-up approach, giving teachers the freedom to craft IDLE programs that address their students' needs and fit their local contexts. By tailoring these programs, IDLE becomes not only more meaningful but also more sustainable over time.

The model organizes learning spaces into four key dimensions using Formality, Location, Pedagogy, and Locus of Control (Benson, 2011b; Reinders & Benson, 2017; Lee, 2019). As discussed earlier, these dimensions create four distinct types of learning environments (Lee, 2024): (a) formal digital learning, (b) nonformal digital learning, (c) extracurricular learning, and (d) extramural learning. This continuum allows teachers to design programs that gradually shift from structured, teacher-controlled environments to more independent, student-driven learning (Liu et al., 2024). For example, Lee (2022a) suggests starting with "weak IDLE" approaches, such as guided extracurricular activities, and progressively moving toward "strong IDLE" practices, where students independently explore digital tools to learn languages.

Research supports the effectiveness of this model. Zhang and Liu (2022), in a study involving 1,080 Chinese EFL students, used structural equation modeling to show how IDLE can help learners transition from extracurricular to extramural contexts. This shift not only increased students' engagement but also boosted their autonomy, demonstrating how the IDLE Continuum Model can effectively bridge the gap between formal and informal learning spaces.

The Teacher-Supported IDLE Continuum Model

The Teacher-Supported IDLE Continuum Model marks a notable step forward from Sundqvist and Sylvén's (2016) influential differentiation between formal and informal language learning. While their foundational research effectively captures the environments and activities – referred to as "extramural" – that foster meaningful informal language development, it does not provide explicit guidance on how educators can systematically cultivate the learner autonomy required for such engagement. Addressing this gap, the Teacher-Supported IDLE Continuum transforms IDLE's descriptive landscape into a practical, pedagogically grounded model. Through the integration of the Gradual Release of Responsibility framework (Pearson & Gallagher, 1983), this model offers educators a clear, structured trajectory to guide learners from reliance on teacher direction toward independent, self-motivated language learning.

Liu et al. (2024), building on this conceptual foundation and leveraging strong collaborations between schools and universities (Sato et al., 2022), have articulated a model that artfully bridges theory and classroom application. Unlike methods that simply introduce learners to digital language resources in hopes of spontaneous growth, the Teacher-Supported IDLE Continuum deliberately scaffolds learner autonomy, ensuring students progressively take ownership of their language journey.

The model is structured into four sequential stages, each aligning with the dimensions of the IDLE model (Liu et al., 2024; see Figure 5):

- **Stage 1 (Teacher-Controlled):** Learning is firmly anchored in traditional classroom dynamics, with teachers curating all materials and directing instruction.
- **Stage 2 (Joint Responsibility):** Responsibility is shared, as learning extends beyond the classroom through collaborative, structured activities that lay the foundations for student autonomy.

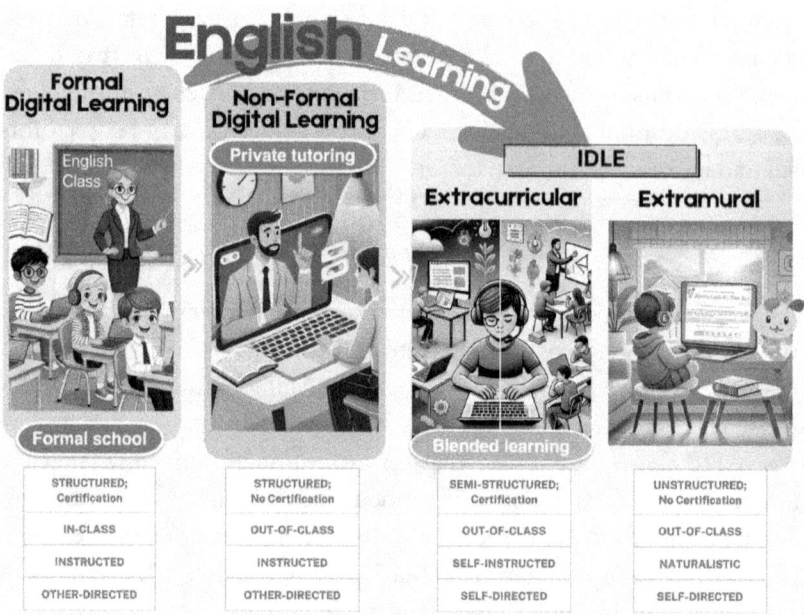

Figure 5 IDLE Continuum Model Pathway

- **Stage 3 (Low Learner-Driven):** Students begin to exercise agency, engaging in semi-structured digital activities that encourage exploration and independent decision-making, thus realizing "weak extramural IDLE."
- **Stage 4 (High Learner-Driven):** Learners achieve full autonomy, leveraging digital resources to pursue self-determined language objectives, embodying "strong extramural IDLE."

A central strength of the continuum is its adaptability across varied educational contexts. Teachers may select the most appropriate entry stage based on their professional judgment and the realities of their institutional settings. For example, educators in innovative or international schools, endowed with greater autonomy and resources, might initiate the process at Stage 3 and advance quickly to Stage 4. Conversely, teachers in more traditional, resource-limited, or hierarchical school settings may choose to begin at Stage 1, gradually transitioning through subsequent stages and selectively incorporating higher stages as conditions permit.

As learners advance through these stages, the teacher's role evolves accordingly:

- **Stage 1:** Teachers act as planners and direct instructors, delivering highly structured lessons.
- **Stages 2 and 3:** The teacher transitions to a facilitator, guiding students through authentic, student-centered digital tasks and fostering critical engagement.
- **Stage 4:** The teacher becomes a mentor, supporting students' reflective practices and helping them continuously refine their strategies for sustained, independent learning.

This phased approach ensures that students are not abruptly thrust into self-directed learning; instead, responsibility is transferred gradually, with continuous support provided as learners build the skills and confidence essential for autonomous, lifelong language learning (Lee, 2024). Evidence from Liu et al. (2024) attests to the model's effectiveness: in a twelve-week intervention involving ninety Chinese EFL university students, those who experienced the full teacher-supported IDLE continuum demonstrated the greatest improvements in willingness to communicate in English, outperforming their peers in both traditional and unsupervised IDLE groups. These findings underscore the indispensable role of educators in scaffolding the path toward learner independence.

In summary, while the IDLE continuum builds on earlier distinctions between extracurricular and extramural learning (Sundqvist, 2009; Sundqvist & Sylvén, 2016), its contribution is not simply terminological.

Rather than presenting parallel categories, the continuum conceptualizes learners' engagement as a developmental trajectory – moving from teacher-supported, structured activities ("weak IDLE") toward fully independent, passion-driven practices ("strong IDLE"). This framing highlights IDLE as a dynamic process rather than a fixed state, and it positions the continuum as both a descriptive tool and a practical tool for guiding transitions across contexts. In this sense, the model is distinctive in linking empirical evidence of learner agency with broader questions of educational and social impact.

4.3 From Academic to Social Impact

Traditionally, the measure of success within academia has relied heavily on quantitative tools, such as citation counts, journal impact factors, and the H-index (Lee, 2025). The H-index, introduced by Hirsch in 2005, tracks how frequently a researcher's work is cited by others, serving as a numerical indicator of their influence and productivity within the scholarly community. These metrics have long been considered the benchmarks for academic achievement, reflecting the extent to which one's work contributes to and is recognized by the field (Lee, 2025).

In recent years, alternative metrics known as *altmetrics* have gained significant traction to gauge a researcher's influence beyond traditional academic circles (Sugimoto et al., 2017). *Altmetrics* measure online engagement through social media mentions, blog posts, news coverage, and other digital platforms. By capturing the attention a piece of research garners in the broader public sphere, *altmetrics* offer a more holistic view of its impact, highlighting how scholarly work resonates with and influences society at large (Sugimoto et al., 2017).

Recognitions, such as inclusion in Stanford/Elsevier's Top 2% Scientist Rankings, further underscore individual achievements in academia (Ioannidis et al., 2019). Being listed among the top scientists signifies that a researcher has made substantial contributions to their field, with work that stands out in terms of innovation, relevance, and citation frequency (Lee, 2025). Such accolades not only honor personal accomplishments but also enhance the visibility of a researcher's work on a global scale.

In applied fields such as language teaching and learning, research has been a driving force behind innovation in areas, such as applied linguistics and Teaching English to Speakers of Other Languages

(TESOL). Scholarly contributions have led to the development of new methodologies, educational technologies, and instructional approaches that address the evolving needs of learners. Leading journals such as *Innovation in Language Learning and Teaching* and influential book series such as *New Language Learning and Teaching Environments* serve as platforms to showcase these advancements. They disseminate cutting-edge research, share best practices, and foster dialogue among educators and researchers dedicated to enhancing language education (Lee, 2025).

However, despite these efforts, critics often point out that academic research often falls short of addressing the real-world challenges faced by educators and learners (Fagerberg et al., 2005; Lee et al., 2025). There is a growing concern that a disconnect exists between theoretical developments and practical application (Sato et al., 2022). Some common limitations highlighted include (Fagerberg et al., 2005; Sato et al., 2022; Lee, 2024, 2025):

- **Lack of connection to real needs:** Research often overlooks the specific and unique challenges of local communities. Scholars may focus on global or generalized issues without considering the cultural, economic, or social contexts that affect how educational strategies are received and implemented at the local level.
- **Issues without relevance and practicality:** Innovations proposed in academic studies may appear promising in theory but fail to meet the practical demands of real-world contexts. Educators and learners might find these solutions impractical due to resource constraints, differing priorities, or logistical challenges inherent in their educational environments.
- **Uncertain long-term impact:** Many solutions lack follow-through, with little attention to their sustainability or lasting value after their initial adoption. Without ongoing support, assessment, and adaptation, interventions introduced by research may diminish over time, limiting their effectiveness and the extent of their benefits.

To address this gap between academic research and societal needs, frameworks such as the United Kingdom's Research Excellence Framework (REF) and Hong Kong's University Grants Committee (UGC) emphasize the importance of research outcomes that extend "beyond academia." Both REF and UGC assess not only the scholarly quality of research but also its tangible impact on policies, practices, and public well-being (Research Excellence Framework, 2021; University Grants Committee, 2023). In this book, social impact is defined as "the demonstrable contributions, beneficial effects, valuable changes or advantages that research qualitatively brings to the economy, society, culture, public policy or services, health, the environment or quality of life; and that are beyond the academia" (University Grants Committee, 2023, p. 20). By measuring research according to its real-world effects, REF and UGC encourage academics to consider the broader significance of their work. Both organizations highlight two main criteria:

- **Reach:** This criterion examines how widely the research benefits individuals and organizations across different sectors. It considers the breadth of influence, assessing whether the research positively impacts a diverse range of communities, industries, and societal groups beyond the immediate academic audience.
- **Significance:** This focuses on the depth of the research's influence on practices, policies, or broader societal understanding. It evaluates the extent to which the research brings about meaningful change, contributes to solving pressing problems, or advances knowledge in a way that has substantial real-world implications.

While the social impact of research is intended to address real-world challenges and improve lives (Smit & Hessels, 2021), there is still no clear framework for approaching language learning and teaching from this angle. The following section introduces a foundational model built around care, innovation, and sustainability.

4.4 Care–Innovation–Sustainability (CIS) Model

The Care–Innovation–Sustainability (CIS) Model (see Figure 6) presents a dynamic, context-sensitive roadmap for weaving innovation into language education (Lee, 2025). It is a holistic and structured approach that champions empathy, school-university collaboration, and long-term impact.

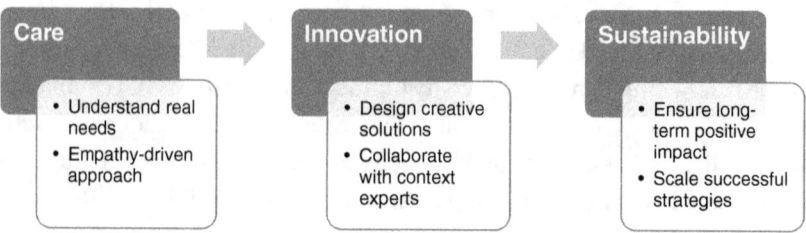

Figure 6 The Care–Innovation–Sustainability Model

Care: Empathy in Action

At the heart of the model is *Care*, which mirrors the "empathy" phase in design thinking (Brown, 2009). This stage is about deeply understanding the unique challenges and needs of beneficiaries (e.g., learners). It goes beyond a simple survey – it demands time, presence, and trust-building (Razzouk & Shute, 2012). Educators must observe, engage, and listen actively to uncover the real, lived experiences of students (Gallagher & Thordarson, 2018). These insights must then be translated into clear, actionable goals. If the problem remains vague or overly complex, it becomes difficult to design meaningful solutions or measure success (Brown, 2009; Lee, 2025).

Innovation: Purposeful and Contextual

Once the needs are clearly defined, *Innovation* takes center stage (Rogers, 2003). This phase introduces new methods or technologies tailored to address the identified challenges (Fagerberg et al., 2005). Crucially, innovation thrives when context experts – such as frontline teachers – are involved (Elliott, 1991; Lee et al., 2025). Their deep understanding of the local environment (e.g., tech infrastructure and school culture) and commitment to change are vital (Hockly, 2014). These experts not only help implement the innovation but also connect researchers with key stakeholders and provide logistical support (Reinders et al., 2025). When universities and schools collaborate, they create a powerful synergy: teachers bring real-world insights and support, while researchers contribute theory, design, and tools to evaluate and refine interventions (Hargreaves & Fullan, 2012; Sato et al., 2022).

Sustainability: Lasting Impact

The final pillar, *Sustainability*, ensures that innovations endure and evolve (Hargreaves & Fullan, 2012). It involves rigorous impact assessment, diverse feedback collection, and strategic scaling (Fowler et al., 2019). Unlike academic projects that rely on limited data, social impact initiatives require a rich mix of evidence – testimonials, classroom observations, and more – to truly gauge effectiveness (Research Excellence Framework, 2021; Smit & Hessels, 2021). Ongoing monitoring helps determine which partnerships to continue and where to focus efforts. This selective approach is key to tracking long-term benefits and refining strategies (Hockly, 2014).

Ultimately, the CIS model aims to transform language education through empathetic, collaborative, and sustainable practices (Fullan, 2007; Lee, 2025). This paradigm shift invites scholars to collaborate more closely with practitioners, policymakers, and the communities they aim to serve (Sato et al., 2022; Sato & Cárcamo, 2024). By doing so, they can develop research initiatives that are grounded in real-world contexts, tailored to specific needs, and designed for long-term viability.

4.5 Integrating the CIS into the IDLE Continuum Model

In under-resourced educational contexts such as Indonesia, English language proficiency is closely linked to the availability of learning opportunities both within and beyond formal schooling (Mitra et al., 2003; Hockly, 2014; Lee et al., 2025). The IDLE model offers a conceptual and pedagogical bridge between home and school environments (Soyoof et al., 2024; Lee et al., 2025). This section illustrates how the CIS model is operationalized within the IDLE continuum, impacting over 2,800 Indonesian students.

Care Phase

Indonesian learners face persistent challenges in acquiring English as a foreign language, particularly in under-resourced settings (Zein, 2017; Lee, 2024). Outside formal education, opportunities for authentic language use are scarce, and socioeconomic constraints further limit access to supplementary learning resources (Lamb, 2004, 2007, 2013; Lee & Drajati, 2019b; Lee, 2024). With an average household income of approximately Indonesian Rupiah 4.2 million (USD 280) per month, many families are unable to afford private tutoring or extracurricular language programs, resulting in restricted exposure to English beyond the classroom (UNICEF, 2020).

Fieldwork conducted in 2024 revealed that students from low-income backgrounds rarely engaged in speaking English, perpetuating cycles of low self-confidence and impeding the development of communicative fluency (Lee, 2024). A comprehensive survey of 2,830 students across more than 20 schools substantiated these observations (Lee, 2024). The data indicated that learners spent less than 1 hour per month on fourteen out of sixteen English-related activities, with productive skills – speaking and writing – receiving minimal attention. In contrast, receptive activities such as listening to English music (69 minutes/month) and using language-learning applications (63 minutes/month) were more prevalent.

Speaking and writing practice averaged under 20 minutes per month, highlighting a critical gap in skill acquisition (Lee, 2024). These findings underscored the urgent need for innovative, scalable, and cost-effective interventions to address the lack of practice and support meaningful improvements in English proficiency (Lee et al., 2025).

From 2020 to 2024, our research team – including Lee, colleagues, graduate students, and Indonesian university partners – laid the groundwork to combat these challenges through strategic partnerships (Sulistyawati, 2025). Collaborations with TEFLIN – The Indonesian Association for English Language Teaching – and Universitas Sebelas Maret (UNS) led to the creation of platforms that trained over 5,500 educators in cutting-edge technology and IDLE methodologies. These initiatives equipped teachers to incorporate IDLE strategies into their classrooms effectively (Lee et al., 2025; Sulistyawati, 2025). In 2024, a renewed five-year Memorandum of Understanding with UNS solidified this ongoing partnership.

Building on similar research into the challenges faced by EFL teachers in Hong Kong (Zadorozhnyy et al., 2025), a pilot study was conducted in March 2024 involving fifty-one Indonesian teachers from over forty schools. The initial results highlighted key obstacles to adopting IDLE techniques, such as a lack of familiarity with the pedagogy (21.3%), challenges in motivating disengaged students (22.2%), and systemic issues such as financial struggles at home (11.1%) and insufficient school infrastructure (10.2%). By grounding the intervention design in the real experiences of Indonesian educators and learners, the Care phase ensured that the solutions developed were not only academically robust but also deeply relevant and sustainable within their specific contexts. This approach set the stage for targeted innovations tailored to meet the urgent needs of underserved communities (Brown, 2009).

Innovation Phase

To expand the reach and deepen the educational impact of the IDLE initiative, a "train-the-trainer" approach was implemented, allowing expertise to spread systematically across the education sector (Marks et al., 2013; Nexø et al., 2024). In the initial phase, fifteen master educators underwent intensive training in IDLE methodologies (Lee, 2024). These master educators then mentored twenty-five frontline teachers from twenty-two schools, who integrated IDLE strategies into their classrooms. Between September and November 2024, this rollout directly impacted 2,820 students (Sulistyawati, 2025). By embedding IDLE activities into everyday lessons, teachers provided students with consistent opportunities to engage with English, significantly increasing language exposure and practice (Lee et al., 2025).

The intervention yielded remarkable results (Lee et al., 2025). Across participating schools, students demonstrated a substantial increase in English engagement. Monthly time spent on receptive skills such as listening and reading jumped from 261 minutes to 510 minutes. Even more striking, time dedicated to productive skills such as speaking and writing surged by 143%, climbing from 234 to 570 minutes per month. Students also experienced emotional and psychological benefits: enjoyment scores rose from 3.67 to 4.50 (out of 5), emotional well-being improved from 3.55 to 4.12, and feelings of boredom decreased from 2.48 to 2.12. Furthermore, communicative confidence and competence advanced significantly, with willingness to speak English increasing from 3.25 to 3.72 and overall perceived communication proficiency improving by over 10 points (from 40.3 to 50.6 out of 100).

These outcomes underscore the effectiveness of IDLE in fostering a positive emotional environment, breaking down psychological barriers, promoting learner autonomy, and developing essential communication skills. The success of the program spurred institutional adoption, with twelve schools officially integrating IDLE into their English curricula, making it a core component of daily instruction (Sulistyawati, 2025).

Case Illustration: Ms. Kiki's Webtoon Revolution

Ms. Kiki, a dedicated frontline teacher, pioneered the use of webtoons as an effective tool for language learning. After attending the International Knowledge Transfer Forum, she explored how informal digital resources like webtoons could support English instruction (Lee et al., 2025). Her journey gained momentum in August 2024 when she participated in a capacity-building workshop focused on integrating IDLE into technology-enhanced classrooms. The workshop emphasized how students naturally engage with English through digital media, encouraging teachers to design interactive, learner-centered lessons.

During the workshop, Ms. Kiki stood out for her active participation. She asked practical questions, shared detailed lesson plans, and provided examples of her teaching strategies through photos saved on her phone. In a follow-up interview, she described IDLE as a framework that aligned with her teaching goals. Her school's support for her innovative methods further enabled her to implement these ideas effectively.

Ms. Kiki's use of webtoons in her classroom had a noticeable impact on her students. Recognizing that many of them spent time reading webtoons after school, she integrated this interest into her lessons. During a site visit, the research team observed how her approach engaged even the quietest students, who enthusiastically discussed their favorite webtoons, using gestures, translanguaging, and peer collaboration to communicate in English.

In one observed lesson:
- **Warm-Up (5 minutes):** Ms. Kiki introduced English-language webtoon platforms and invited students to share their favorite webtoons. One student, with limited English vocabulary, managed to describe her chosen story using gestures and peer support, showing determination to express herself in English.
- **Group Work (30 minutes):** Students worked in teams to debate characters and plot twists, actively exchanging ideas.
- **Presentation (10 minutes):** Groups presented summaries of their favorite webtoons, and for homework, students were asked to write an essay analyzing their chosen webtoon.

Students credited Ms. Kiki's approach with increasing their motivation and making English learning more relevant to their interests. By incorporating webtoons, she created opportunities for meaningful engagement with the language in a context familiar to her learners. Ms. Kiki's work demonstrates how educators can use informal digital media to make language learning relatable and effective. Her approach highlights the potential of IDLE to foster engagement, support learner autonomy, and encourage authentic language use.

Sustainability Phase

Between January and May 2025, the IDLE initiative entered its consolidation phase, focusing on eight schools and seven highly committed educators. What began in spring 2024 with training over 100 teachers was narrowed down to 25 by summer 2024 when the program launched, and ultimately to a core group of 7 educators who demonstrated unwavering dedication and were strongly supported by their schools and leadership. This phase marked the introduction of a rigorous experimental research design – developed in collaboration with Indonesian partners – that included control groups to generate robust evidence of the program's effectiveness. While data analysis is still ongoing, preliminary findings offer valuable insights into the initiative's sustainability.

The selection of the seven teachers was a deliberate process shaped by real-world constraints. Initially, around 100 teachers expressed interest in the program. However, challenges such as personal health, limited access to technology, and administrative workloads led many to withdraw (Ruspini, 2002). The remaining seven educators stood out for their high commitment, building strong professional relationships with the research team through ongoing training, informal conversations, and school-based observations. This trust-based collaboration has set the stage for a longitudinal study to assess the program's sustained impact (Melnyk & Morrison-Beedy, 2012).

To enhance the methodological rigor, the team adopted Experience Sampling Method (ESM), allowing real-time data collection on students' engagement with IDLE activities (Arndt et al., 2023; Lee & Chiu, 2024). This approach provided more reliable and detailed insights. Along with pre- and post-surveys, the research team gathered diverse evidence, including classroom observations, teacher interviews, testimonials, and local media coverage. This multidimensional data offers a comprehensive view of the program's social impact (Sulistyawati, 2025), strengthening the case for scaling IDLE to other regions in Indonesia and similar contexts in the Global South (Research Excellence Framework, 2021).

Capacity building remained central to the initiative. Graduate students from Indonesia and Hong Kong participated actively in the project, gaining hands-on experience in community-based research and collaborative methodologies (Lee, 2024). This involvement not only enhanced their academic and research skills but also empowered them to lead future social impact projects. For instance, one doctoral student is currently writing her dissertation based on her work with the initiative. Upon graduation, she is expected to lead similar projects, amplifying the program's influence and fostering a ripple effect among educators, researchers, and emerging scholars.

A significant lesson learned during this phase was the strategic use of technology. Initially, the team partnered with a commercial AI provider to assess students' speaking fluency. While this generated excitement at first, both teachers and students faced challenges with the product's complexity and inaccuracies. For researchers, the high cost of the tool was another barrier. These experiences highlighted the need for affordable, user-friendly, and contextually appropriate technologies (Hockly, 2014; Lee, 2024). As a result, the team is now developing AI-mediated IDLE using free, open-source tools in collaboration with an ed-tech company based in the Global South, ensuring greater accessibility and alignment with local needs (Kim, 2009).

Institutional engagement played a crucial role in reinforcing the program's sustainability (Melnyk and Morrison-Beedy, 2012). A dedicated forum brought together key stakeholders, including a senior advisor to the Indonesian Minister of Education, the president of TEFLIN, and representatives from an NGO school network (Sulistyawati, 2025). These discussions explored pathways for policy integration, laying the groundwork for governmental endorsement and the potential inclusion of IDLE in the national curriculum. Institutional support not only validates the program's effectiveness but also paves the way for systemic reform in English language education across Indonesia (Lee, 2025).

5 Future Directions for IDLE

This section envisions how IDLE can evolve and flourish in the coming years, driven by new practices, fresh research, and broader community engagement. It highlights five promising pathways for growth: (a) reaching new populations and settings – including those where languages other than English (LOTE) are spoken; (b) exploring a wider range of conceptual frameworks to enrich IDLE; (c) pioneering innovative research methods; (d) weaving IDLE more deeply into school environments; and (e) harnessing IDLE's potential for meaningful social impact. Each direction aims to broaden, deepen, and elevate IDLE's role in language education and beyond.

5.1 Expanding Horizons: New Populations and Contexts

IDLE research has gained momentum over the past five years, with studies spanning more than ten regions around the globe – from Hong Kong and Iran to Indonesia and Sweden (Lee, 2022a; Dressman et al., 2023; Soyoof et al., 2023). Yet, much of this work zeroes in on university and high school students in European and Asian EFL settings (Soyoof et al., 2023; Kusyk et al., 2025). To capture the full landscape of IDLE, future research needs to reach beyond these boundaries, delving into a richer variety of age groups, cultures, and communities whose stories with IDLE have yet to be told.

A significant blind spot remains: the Global South (Lamb, 2004, 2007, 2013; Farid & Lamb, 2020; Lee et al., 2025). The Global South is not just a geographic or economic label – it is a crucial perspective that challenges Western-centric viewpoints and amplifies the voices of communities that have often been overlooked (Pennycook & Makoni, 2019). This includes not only large parts of Africa, Asia, Latin America, and the Middle East, but also marginalized groups within the Global North itself

(Dressman et al., 2016; Liu & Darvin, 2023; Lee, 2024, 2025; Soyoof et al., 2024; Rezai et al., 2025). Advancing the field means investigating how learners in these regions engage with IDLE, often in the face of limited resources, complex multilingual realities, and deeply rooted heritage languages (Hockly, 2014; Guo & Lee, 2023; McCallum & Tafazoli, 2024). For many, digital language learning is not just a matter of access – it is a powerful story of resilience and ingenuity, where creative learner strategies turn challenges into opportunities (Dressman et al., 2016; Lee & Drajati, 2019a, 2019b; Liu & Darvin, 2023; Lee, 2024).

While evidence shows that both adolescents and young adults can benefit from digital language learning, we know less about how children and adults uniquely experience and interact with IDLE (Sylvén & Sundqvist, 2012; Jensen, 2017, 2019; Cheung, 2023; Soyoof et al., 2024; Kusyk et al., 2025). Exploring their distinct habits and motivations could unlock a wealth of new insights (Jensen, 2019; Cheung, 2023). Comparative research across different cultures and education systems can further reveal how demographics and local contexts shape IDLE practices, equipping educators to design more relevant and effective approaches (Lee & Sylvén, 2021; Guo & Lee, 2023; Rezai et al., 2025; Zou et al., 2025).

The field is also beginning to embrace informal digital language learning for languages beyond English. Recent studies have shown Chinese university students informally learning French and German via digital tools (Liu et al., 2024); others have highlighted the role of AI in supporting learners of English and Japanese (Guo & Xia, 2025), and American students using digital means to pick up Chinese, French, Russian, and Spanish (Lin, 2023). There is also a surge of interest in learning Korean online around the world (Isbell, 2018; Hiromi, 2023; Lee, Y.-J., 2023; Lee, Kiaer, & Jeong, 2025). These findings demonstrate IDLE's flexibility and its growing relevance for LOTE. As digital technologies continue to advance, there will be even more chances to explore how learners skillfully juggle multiple languages in ever-changing online spaces (Liu et al., 2024). By welcoming a wider spectrum of learners and contexts, future IDLE research can deepen our understanding of digital language learning everywhere – paving the way for greater innovation, inclusion, and equity (Sundqvist, 2022; Guo & Lee, 2023; Lee, 2024; Liu et al., 2025).

5.2 Deepening IDLE: Systematic Reviews and Diverse Conceptual Frameworks

As IDLE research has evolved, scholars have adopted a rich array of analytical methods to chart the field's development. Systematic reviews have been pivotal in this process. For example, Soyoof et al. (2023) conducted a scoping review, examining four decades of research into the linguistic, cultural, emotional, and digital literacy dimensions of IDLE across Asia and Europe. Similarly, Kusyk et al. (2025) broadened the lens with a scoping review of informal second language learning practices from 2000 to 2020. By contrast, Liu et al. (2025) offered a more focused thematic review, zeroing in on IDLE in Asian EFL contexts, while Aiju et al. (2025) mapped the growth of IDLE research from 1998 to 2024 through a systematic and bibliometric analysis.

Different perspectives have added further richness. Guo and Lee (2023), for instance, applied Bronfenbrenner's ecological framework to explore how personal and environmental factors jointly shape learners' experiences with IDLE. Lee (2022b) contributed a systematic methodological review, critiquing seventy-six studies and highlighting opportunities to refine research methods in the field. Dressman et al. (2025) used a cross-case analytic approach (Wittgenstein, 1958; Monk, 2005), drawing on forty-seven narratives from twenty-nine ethnographic studies of informal language learners between 2000 and 2020. Their findings revealed how time, space, and ongoing formal instruction intertwine with informal language learning, and how ethnographic, multi-case studies can capture both broad patterns and nuanced, deeply contextualized experiences. Other studies, such as Zhang et al. (2021), have mapped the broader landscape of extramural language learning, while Guan et al. (2024) used meta-analysis to show the positive impact of AI-powered IDLE on learning outcomes. This blend of systematic, scoping, thematic, and meta-analytic reviews demonstrates that IDLE has matured into a vibrant and multifaceted domain.

From these reviews, new directions are taking shape as researchers explore IDLE through a variety of conceptual lenses. They have considered factors such as formality, location, pedagogy, and locus of control (Benson, 2011b), each offering unique insights into the complexities of informal digital language learning (Lee, 2019, 2022a). Liu et al. (2024) investigated the intersection of AI and IDLE, introducing the concept of AI-mediated IDLE through the technology acceptance model. This line of inquiry has since grown to include studies on GenAI-IDLE, which use self determination theory to delve into what motivates learners (Wu & Wang, 2025).

The diversity of IDLE activities has also prompted new ways of categorizing them. Some researchers distinguish between form-focused activities, such as vocabulary and grammar drills, and meaning-focused practices, such as watching videos or joining online conversations (Lee, 2019; Zou et al., 2025). More recently, Lee, Xie, and Lee (2024) expanded these categories to include game-based learning and to differentiate between productive (content creation) and receptive (content consumption) engagement.

Looking ahead, as more reviews of IDLE accumulate in the field, researchers can diversify their approaches to systematic analysis. They might consider methodological reviews (Chong & Reinders, 2021), meta-reviews or umbrella reviews (Chang et al., 2025), narrative reviews (Peng et al., 2021), critical reviews (Credé, 2018), and qualitative research syntheses (Chong & Plonsky, 2021) to capture different dimensions and nuances of IDLE research. Future studies could also explore emerging forms of IDLE – such as language learning through chatbots, dating apps, mobile games, or even e-commerce platforms – drawing from an array of theoretical perspectives. These innovative directions promise to further enrich our understanding of how digital tools and ever-evolving online spaces are transforming informal language learning around the world.

5.3 Innovating IDLE Methodologies

In contrast to traditional second language acquisition studies – which typically unfold in the controlled confines of classrooms or labs – IDLE research often ventures into the vibrant, unpredictable spaces where language learning naturally happens (Lee, 2022a). To truly understand these authentic experiences, researchers are advised to embrace new approaches. However, much of the existing work still relies on retrospective tools, such as surveys and interviews. For instance, Lee (2022b) analyzed seventy-six studies on Language Learning and Teaching Beyond the Classroom (LBC), which includes IDLE, from 2010 to 2020. The review highlighted a heavy dependence on conventional methods such as questionnaires, interviews, and observations, while richer, more nuanced approaches – such as language logs, group interviews, reflective journals, computer tracking, stimulated recall, and personal learning histories – were rarely used.

Fortunately, as technology advances and the field matures, researchers are increasingly experimenting with innovative, cross-disciplinary methods (Lee, 2024). To overcome the challenge of unreliable self-reports and the risk of participants exaggerating their learning behaviors (Mortel, 2008), researchers are increasingly triangulating data sources – combining surveys with interviews, language logs, and computer tracking (Lai & Gu, 2011; Nielson, 2011; Sylvén & Sundqvist, 2012; Toetenel, 2014; Sundqvist, 2024). Sundqvist (2009), for example, used diary studies across weeks, averaging results for greater accuracy. Vazquez-Calvo et al. (2019) leveraged screen recordings of IDLE activities, providing vivid, context-rich evidence that can be paired with stimulated recall interviews to offer deeper, real-time insights.

One promising innovation is the tracking app, designed to help learners log informal language activities easily and precisely (Arndt et al., 2022). Another promising technique is the "ESM," often used in psychology (Parson & Csikszentmihalyi, 2014), where researchers send multiple daily prompts – sometimes through social media – over a week or two to capture real-time snapshots of learners' IDLE behaviors (Arndt et al., 2023; Reinders & Lee, 2023; Lee & Chiu, 2024).

When it comes to analyzing data, IDLE research has traditionally leaned on descriptive and correlational statistics, which do not always reveal direct cause-and-effect connections between IDLE and language learning outcomes (Kusyk et al., 2025). While advanced approaches like "structural equation modeling" help map relationships in large datasets, they still fall short of experimental rigor (Lee & Chiu, 2023; Kusyk et al., 2025). To build a stronger evidence base, researchers are encouraged to incorporate quasi-experimental and experimental designs, even though these can be logistically challenging (Kusyk et al., 2025). Design-based research stands out as a practical way to assess how IDLE initiatives affect both students and educators (Lee et al., 2025).

Acknowledging the complexity and individuality of IDLE (Godwin-Jones, 2018), future studies could take a person-centered approach, using cluster analysis or Q-methodology to unveil unique learner patterns (Peng, Jager, & Lowie, 2022; Lee & Xie, 2023; Guo & Xia, 2025; Guo et al., 2025; Lai & Wang, 2025). For example, Peng, Lowie, and Jager (2022) utilized time-series clustering to follow the evolving IDLE habits of Chinese EFL students, offering a detailed, dynamic perspective on their learning journeys. Similarly, Guo and Xia (2025) employed Q-methodology to explore students' attitudes toward AI-driven multilingual learning, highlighting shared beliefs within various groups.

5.4 Integrating IDLE into Education: From K-12 to University

The growth of digital technologies (e.g., GenAI) has transformed the ways EFL learners encounter and use English outside the classroom (Richards, 2015; Liu et al., 2024a; Kusyk et al., 2025). In response, a surge of research has spotlighted the advantages of IDLE or informal language learning, sparking widespread calls to integrate it into mainstream education. These calls echo across academic articles (Godwin-Jones, 2019), books (Sundqvist & Sylvén, 2016; Dressman & Sadler, 2020), book chapters (Hubbard, 2020), research agenda papers (Lai & Sundqvist, 2025), practical teacher handbooks (Dressman et al., 2023; Lee et al., 2024), seminars (Arndt & Lyrigkou, 2019), and even international symposiums (Lee & Chik, 2025).

At the university level, some educators have pioneered concrete methods for embedding IDLE into higher education. For instance, Lee (2024) co-created an interdisciplinary course titled 'Informal Learning of Digital Natives.' In this course, students tackled a two-week informal learning challenge, setting SMART (Specific, Measurable, Achievable, Relevant, Time-bound) goals and leveraging a variety of digital tools and psychological strategies (Doran, 1981). Early results were encouraging: students honed their language skills by analyzing YouTube content or crafting original social media posts. Their progress was captured through reflective videos and detailed essays, where they charted their journey, from initial aims to achievements, setbacks, and plans for the future.

In contrast, K–12 schools – particularly those in exam-driven Asian systems – often face significant hurdles when trying to integrate IDLE into their curricula (Guo & Lee, 2023). Drawing on Bronfenbrenner's ecological systems theory, Guo and Lee (2023) revealed how larger systemic pressures shape students' opportunities for informal learning. Similarly, Zadorozhnyy et al. (2025) documented the struggles of Hong Kong teachers, who found it difficult to embed IDLE activities amid rigid syllabi and heavy workloads, even when teacher educators were supportive. To navigate these constraints, Lee (2022a) advocates for a "compromised pedagogy" – a flexible, context-sensitive approach that adapts the frequency and type of IDLE activities to fit the realities of each school. In particularly restrictive environments, this might mean only occasional informal activities; where there is more flexibility, regular integration becomes possible.

Some researchers have demonstrated how this adaptable approach works in practice. Sundqvist and Sylvén (2016) suggested ways to bring "extramural English" into schools, inspiring Lee and a team of Hong Kong secondary teachers to launch a fourteen-day Extramural English challenge using Padlet during the pandemic (Lee, 2024). Students set individual learning goals and tracked their progress, which proved especially valuable for shy or introverted learners, nurturing a sense of community, independence, and emotional well-being. The response was highly positive – many students continued their engagement well after the challenge ended. At the primary level, Lee (2024) partnered with teachers to introduce hands-on IDLE strategies, such as using Google Assistant for language practice. In one case, a teacher designed special worksheets and assigned Google Assistant activities as homework to help students master challenging English sounds like /b/ and /p/. This approach empowered students to practice and build confidence on their own, boosting both their skills and motivation.

Looking forward, building strong partnerships between researchers and classroom teachers offers the most promising path (Sato et al., 2022). Teachers bring practical, day-to-day knowledge about what engages students, while researchers provide fresh theories and innovative resources. For instance, digital games have delivered impressive gains in vocabulary and speaking skills in Nordic classrooms (Sundqvist, 2009, 2019), but these approaches need thoughtful adaptation to fit the exam-driven realities of Asian EFL schools (Lee & Sylvén, 2021). By codesigning IDLE strategies tailored to local contexts, educators and researchers can ensure these innovations are not only effective but also relevant and sustainable for their communities.

5.5 Using IDLE for Social Impact

As the field of IDLE continues to grow, its profound influence on lifelong learning (Sundqvist, 2022) and overall well-being (Lee & Chiu, 2024) is becoming increasingly evident. These positive impacts closely mirror the aims of global initiatives like UNESCO's Sustainable Development Goals – especially Goal 3 (promoting health and well-being) and Goal 4 (ensuring quality education for all). The capacity of IDLE to drive social transformation unlocks fresh opportunities to tackle global issues and inform more effective policies and educational practices (Lee et al., 2025). By embracing IDLE, educators and policymakers could address pressing social needs that extend well beyond traditional academic boundaries.

However, a significant obstacle remains: the growing digital divide – the gap between those with reliable access to up-to-date technologies and those without (Warschauer, 2003). This divide leads to marked disparities in who can actually participate in and benefit from IDLE (Godwin-Jones, 2021; Guo & Lee, 2023; McCallum & Tafazoli, 2024). Students lacking stable internet or digital devices are too often sidelined, missing valuable chances to enhance their language skills and access crucial educational resources (Hockly, 2014; Lee, 2024). These inequities only deepen existing divides in education (Sundqvist, 2022). To create a more just learning landscape, researchers are encouraged to investigate these challenges and develop targeted, locally relevant solutions that address the day-to-day realities faced by learners and educators in marginalized and under-resourced communities (Lee et al., 2025).

References

Aiju, L., Abdullah, A., & Yufeng, W. (2025). Informal learning of English or English learning beyond the classroom? A systematic and bibliometric review (1998–2024). *International Journal of Instruction, 18*(2), 261–284. https://files.eric.ed.gov/fulltext/EJ1341731.pdf

Alhaq, M. N. D. (2022). Playing games during pandemic, why not? The IDLE upon students' efficacy and vocabulary. *Indonesian Journal of Applied Linguistics, 12*(1), 180–200. https://doi.org/10.17509/ijal.v12i1.46536

Arndt, H. L., Granfeldt, J., & Gullberg, M. (2022). The Lang-Track-App: Open-source tools for implementing the experience sampling method in second language acquisition research. *Language Learning*, 1–35. https://doi.org/10.1111/lang.12555

Arndt, H. L., Granfeldt, J., & Gullberg, M. (2023). Reviewing the potential of the Experience Sampling Method (ESM) for capturing second language exposure and use. *Second Language Research, 39*(1), 39–58. https://doi.org/10.1177/02676583211020055

Arndt, H. L., & Lyrigkou, C. (2019). (In)Formal L2 learning: Integrating informal practices into formal contexts. *Language Teaching, 52*, 415–417. https://doi.org/10.1017/S026144481900017X

Arndt, H. L., & Woore, R. (2018). Vocabulary learning from watching YouTube videos and reading blog posts. *Language Learning & Technology, 22*(3), 124–142. https://doi.org/10125/44660

Bandura, A. (1997). *Self-efficacy: The exercise of control*. W. H. Freeman.

Barkati, M., Kiyanfar, Z., Noughabi, M. A., & Ershadi, F. (2024). Contributions of self-efficacy, L2 grit and digital literacy to informal digital learning of English: A structural equation modelling approach. *British Journal of Educational Technology*, 1–19. https://doi.org/10.1111/bjet.13547

Becker, D. (2022). On the use of commercial video games in the EFL classroom in North Rhine-Westphalia – An empirical perspective. *Anglistik, 33*(1), 59–75. https://doi.org/10.33675/ANGL/2022/1/8

Benson, P. (2011a). *Teaching and researching autonomy in language learning* (2nd ed.). Longman.

Benson, P. (2011b). Language learning and teaching beyond the classroom: An introduction to the field. In P. Benson & H. Reinders (Eds.), *Beyond the language classroom* (pp. 7–16). Palgrave Macmillan.

Bronfenbrenner, U. (1976). The experimental ecology of education. *Educational Researcher, 5*(9), 5–15.

Bronfenbrenner, U. (1979). *The ecology of human development: Experiments by nature and design*. Harvard University Press.

Brown, T. (2009). *Change by design: How design thinking transforms organizations and inspires innovation*. HarperBusiness.

Bruen, J., & Erdocia, I. (2024). Formal and informal foreign language learning at university: Blurring the boundaries. *The Language Learning Journal*, 1–14. https://doi.org/10.1080/09571736.2024.2306157

Buechner, V. L., Pekrun, R., & Lichtenfeld, S. (2018). The Achievement Pride Scales (APS). *European Journal of Psychological Assessment*, *34*(3), 181–192. https://doi.org/10.1027/1015-5759/a000325

Butler, Y. G. (2015). The use of computer games as foreign language learning tasks for digital natives. *System*, *54*, 91–102. https://doi.org/10.1016/j.system.2014.10.010

Chang, Y.-K., Ren, F.-F., Li, R.-H., Ai, J.-Y., Kao, S.-C., & Etnier, J. L. (2025). Effects of acute exercise on cognitive function: A meta-review of 30 systematic reviews with meta-analyses. *Psychological Bulletin*, *151*(2), 240–259. https://doi.org/10.1037/bul0000460

Chen, C. W.-y. (2020). Learning through participation: A case study on the affordances of making YouTube tutorial videos. *The JALT CALL Journal*, *16*(1), 51–67. https://doi.org/10.29140/jaltcall.v16n1.259

Cheung, A. (2023). Young adolescents' out-of-class language learning and their degree of autonomy: Insights from visual and verbal narratives. *Innovation in Language Learning and Teaching*, *17*(5), 909–931. https://doi.org/10.1080/17501229.2023.2195381

Chik, A. (2014). Digital gaming and language learning: Autonomy and community. *Language Learning & Technology*, *18*(2), 85–100.

Chik, A., & Ho, J. (2017). Learn a language for free: Recreational learning among adults. *System*, *69*, 162–171. https://doi.org/10.1016/j.system.2017.07.017

Chong, S. W., & Plonsky, L. (2021). A primer on qualitative research synthesis in TESOL. *TESOL Quarterly*, *55*(3), 1024–1034. https://doi.org/10.1002/tesq.3030

Chong, S. W., & Reinders, H. (2021). A methodological review of qualitative research syntheses in CALL: The state-of-the-art. *System*, *103*, 1–15. https://doi.org/10.1016/j.system.2021.102646

Chun, D. (2016). The role of technology in SLA research. *Language Learning & Technology*, *20*(2), 98–115. https://doi.org/10125/44463

Chun, D. (2019). Current and future directions in TELL. *Educational Technology & Society*, *22*(2), 14–25. www.jstor.org/stable/26891614

Cole, J., & Vanderplank, R. (2016). Comparing autonomous and class-based learners in Brazil: Evidence for the present-day advantages of informal, out-of-class learning. *System*, *61*, 31–42. https://doi.org/10.1016/j.system.2016.07.007

Credé, M. (2018). What shall we do about grit? A critical review of what we know and what we don't know. *Educational Researcher*, *47*(9), 606–611. https://doi.org/10.3102/0013189X18801322

Crystal, D. (2010). *The Cambridge encyclopedia of language*. Cambridge University Press.

Csikszentmihalyi, M. (2014). *Flow and the foundations of positive psychology: The collected works of Mihaly Csikszentmihalyi*. Springer.

Deci, E. L., & Ryan, R. M. (1985). *Intrinsic motivation and self-determination in human behavior* (2nd ed.). Plenum Press.

Dewaele, J.-M., & MacIntyre, P. D. (2014). The two faces of Janus? Anxiety and enjoyment in the foreign language classroom. *Studies in Second Language Learning and Teaching*, *4*(2), 237–274. https://doi.org/10.14746/ssllt.2014.4.2.5

Dewaele, J.-M., & MacIntyre, P. D. (2016). Foreign language enjoyment and foreign language classroom anxiety. The right and left feet of FL learning? In P. D. MacIntyre, T. Gregersen, & S. Mercer (Eds.), *Positive psychology in SLA* (pp. 215–236). Multilingual Matters.

De Wilde, V., Brysbaert, M., & Eyckmans, J. (2022). Formal versus informal L2 learning: How do individual differences and word-related variables influence French and English L2 vocabulary learning in Dutch-Speaking children? *Studies in Second Language Acquisition*, *44*(1), 87–111. https://doi.org/10.1017/S0272263121000097

Dizon, G. (2023). Foreign language learning in the digital wilds: A qualitative research synthesis. *CALICO Journal*, *40*(2), 238–256. https://doi.org/10.1558/cj.22360

Dooly, M., & Sadler, R. (2013). Filling in the gaps: Linking theory and practice through telecollaboration in teacher education. *ReCALL*, *25*(1), 4–29. https://doi.org/10.1017/S0958344012000237

Doran, G. T. (1981). There's a S.M.A.R.T way to write management's goals and objectives. *Management Review*, *70*(11), 35–36.

Dörnyei, Z. (2009). The L2 motivational self system. In Z. Dörnyei & E. Ushioda (Eds.), *Motivation, language identity and the L2 self* (pp. 9–42). Multilingual Matters.

Dressman, M., & Lee, J. S. (2021). IDLE in the classroom: Learner-driven strategies for English language learning. *The Clearing House*, *94*(4), 181–187. https://doi.org/10.1080/00098655.2021.1929802

Dressman, M., Lee, J. S., & Perrot, L. (2023). *English language learning in the digital age: Learner-driven strategies for adolescents and young adults.* Wiley-Blackwell.

Dressman, M., Lee, J. S., & Sabaoui, M. A. (2016). Path to English in Korea: Policies, practices, and outcomes. *English Language Teaching, 28*(1), 67–78. https://doi.org/10.17936/pkelt.2016.28.1.4

Dressman, M., & Sadler, R. (Eds.). (2020). *The handbook of informal language learning.* Wiley-Blackwell.

Dressman, M., Toffoli, D., & Lee, J. S. (2025). Developing a cross-case, time-ordered analysis of informal language learning from ethnographic narratives. *Research Methods in Applied Linguistics, 4,* 100190. https://doi.org/10.1016/j.rmal.2025.100190

Duckworth, A. L. (2017). *Grit: Why passion and resilience are the secrets to success.* Ebury Publishing.

Dweck, C. S. (2000). *Self-theories: Their role in motivation, personality, and development.* Taylor & Francis Group.

Elliott, J. (1991). *Action research for educational change.* Open University Press.

Fagerberg, J., Mowery, D. C., & Nelson, R. R. (Eds.). (2005). *The Oxford handbook of innovation.* Oxford University Press.

Farid, A., & Lamb, M. (2020). English for Da'wah? L2 motivation in Indonesian pesantren schools. *System, 94,* 1–13. https://doi.org/10.1016/j.system.2020.102310

Fathali, S., & Okada, T. (2018). Technology acceptance model in technology-enhanced OCLL contexts: A self-determination theory approach. *Australasian Journal of Educational Technology, 34*(4), 138–154. https://doi.org/10.14742/ajet.3629

Fowler, E. A. R., Coffey, B. S., & Dixon-Fowler, H. R. (2019). Transforming good intentions into social impact: A case on the creation and evolution of a social enterprise. *Journal of Business Ethics, 159,* 665–678. https://doi.org/10.1007/s10551-017-3754-5

Friedman, T. L. (2005). *The world is flat: A brief history of the twenty-first century.* Farrar, Straus and Giroux.

Fu, R. (2025). Enjoyment and grit as mediators between informal digital learning English, basic psychology needs, and willingness to communicate among English as a foreign language university students. *Current Psychology,* 1–15. https://doi.org/10.1007/s12144-024-07220-w

Fullan, M. (2007). *The new meaning of educational change.* Teachers College Press.

Funada, N. (2024). Effects of students' contact with the English language and its users on students' preferences for Global Englishes Language Teaching. *TESOL Quarterly*, 1–28. https://doi.org/10.1002/tesq.3363

Gallagher, A., & Thordarson, K. (2018). *Design thinking for school leaders*. ASCD.

Gao, Y., Wang, X., & Reynolds, B. L. (2025). The mediating roles of resilience and flow in linking basic psychological needs to tertiary EFL learners' engagement in the informal digital learning of English: A mixed-methods study. *Behavioral Sciences*, *15*(1), 1–21. https://doi.org/10.3390/bs15010085

Ghasemi, A., & Noughabi, M. A. (2024). Investigating the mediating role of foreign language peace of mind and learning burnout in the relationship between informal digital learning of English and willingness to communicate. *Computer Assisted Language Learning*, 1–30. https://doi.org/10.1080/09588221.2024.2424321

Godwin-Jones, R. (2016). Looking back and ahead: 20 years of technologies for language learning. *Language Learning & Technology*, *20*(2), 5–12.

Godwin-Jones, R. (2018). Chasing the butterfly effect: Informal language learning online as a complex system. *Language Learning & Technology*, *22*(2), 8–27. https://doi.org/10125/44643

Godwin-Jones, R. (2019). In a world of SMART technology, why learn another language? *Educational Technology & Society*, *22*(2), 4–13.

Godwin-Jones, R. (2020). Future directions in informal language learning. In M. Dressman & R. Sadler (Eds.), *The handbook of informal language learning*. Wiley-Blackwell.

Godwin-Jones, R. (2021). Evolving technologies for language learning. *Language Learning & Technology*, *25*(3), 6–26. https://doi.org/10125/73443

Godwin-Jones, R. (2022). Partnering with AI: Intelligent writing assistance and instructed language learning. *Language Learning & Technology*, *26*(2), 5–24. https://doi.org/10125/73474

Graddol, D. (2006). *English next: Why global English may mean the end of 'English as a foreign language'*. British Council.

Guan, L., Li, S., & Gu, M. M. (2024). AI in informal digital English learning: A meta-analysis of its effectiveness on proficiency, motivation, and self-regulation. *Computers and Education: Artificial Intelligence*, *7*, 1–9. https://doi.org/10.1016/j.caeai.2024.100323

Guan, L., Zhang, E. Y., & Gu, M. M. (2024). Examining generative AI-mediated informal digital learning of English practices with social cognitive theory: A mixed-methods study. *ReCALL*, 1–17. https://doi.org/10.1017/S0958344024000259

Guo, S., & Xia, M. (2025). Exploring learners' perceptions of AI-mediated informal digital multilingual learning: A Q-methodology approach. *International Journal of Applied Linguistics*, 1–13. https://doi.org/10.1111/ijal.12815

Guo, S., Yao, H., & Lee, J. S. (2025). A latent profile analysis of informal digital learning of English: Emotion regulation strategies as predictors and willingness to communicate as outcomes. *System, 132*, 103686. https://doi.org/10.1016/j.system.2025.103686

Guo, X., & Lee, J. S. (2023). A systematic review of Informal Digital Learning of English: An ecological systems theory perspective. *System, 117*, 1–14. https://doi.org/10.1016/j.system.2023.103097

Hargreaves, A., & Fullan, M. (2012). *Professional capital: Transforming teaching in every school.* Teachers College Press.

Hiromi, N. (2023). My Korean language teachers are YouTubers: Learning Korean via self-instruction. *Computer Assisted Language Learning, 36*(3), 346–374. https://doi.org/10.1080/09588221.2021.1928227

Hirsch, J. E. (2005). An index to quantify an individual's scientific research output. *PNAS 102*(46), 16569–16572. https://doi.org/10.1073/pnas.0507655102.

Hockly, N. (2014). Digital technologies in low-resource ELT contexts. *ELT Journal, 68*(1), 79–84. https://doi.org/10.1093/elt/cct063

Hubbard, P. (2020). Leveraging technology to integrate informal language learning within classroom settings. In M. Dressman & R. Sadler (Eds.), *The handbook of informal language learning* (pp. 405–419). Wiley-Blackwell.

Hwang, G.-J., & Lai, C.-L. (2017). Facilitating and bridging out-of-class and in-class learning: An interactive e-book-based flipped learning approach for Math courses. *Educational Technology & Society, 20*(1), 184–197.

Ioannidis, J. P. A., Baas, J., Klavans, R., & Boyack, K. W. (2019). A standardized citation metrics author database annotated for scientific field. *PLOS Biology, 17*(8), 1–6. https://doi.org/10.1371/journal.pbio.3000384

Isbell, D. R. (2018). Online informal language learning: Insights from a Korean learning community. *Language Learning & Technology, 22*(3), 82–102. https://doi.org/10125/44658/

Jenkins, H., Purushotma, R., Weigel, M., Clinton, K., & Robison, A. J. (2009). *Confronting the challenges of participatory culture: Media education for the 21st century.* The MIT Press.

Jensen, S. H. (2017). Gaming as an English language learning resource among young children in Denmark. *CALICO Journal, 34*(1), 1–19. https://doi.org/10.1558/cj.29519

Jensen, S. H. (2019). Language learning in the wild: A young user perspective. *Language Learning & Technology, 23*(1), 72–86. https://doi.org/10125/44673

Jeon, J. (2022). Exploring a self-directed interactive app for informal EFL learning: A self-determination theory perspective. *Education and Information Technologies, 27*, 5767–5787. https://doi.org/10.1007/s10639-021-10839-y

Kaatari, H., Larsson, T., Wang, Y., & Acikara-Eickhoff, S. (2023). Exploring the effects of target-language extramural activities on students' written production. *Journal of Second Language Writing, 62*, 1–12. https://doi.org/10.1016/j.jslw.2023.101062

Kaplan-Rakowski, R., Lin, L., & Wojdynski, T. (2021). Learning vocabulary using 2D pictures is more effective than using immersive 3D steroscopic pictures. *International Journal of Human-Computer Interaction*, 1–10. https://doi.org/10.1080/10447318.2021.1938394

Kelley, T. L. (1927). *Interpretation of educational measurements*. World Book Company.

Kim, H. (2015). Technology and language learning research in English Teaching: Critical reflections and future directions. *English Teaching, 70*(5), 355–379. https://doi.org/10.15858/engtea.

Kim, P. (2009). Action research approach on mobile learning design for the underserved. *Educational Technology Research and Development, 57*, 415–435. https://doi.org/10.1007/s11423-008-9109-2

Kusuma, I. P. I., Dewi, N. L. P. E. S., & Paramartha, A. A. G. Y. (2024). Informal digital learning of English to support a formal speaking course: EFL preservice teachers' perceptions and implementation ideas. *Turkish Online Journal of Distance Education, 25*(4), 244–259. https://doi.org/10.17718/tojde.1360065

Kusyk, M. (2017). The development of complexity, accuracy and fluency in L2 written production through informal participation in online activities. *CALICO Journal, 34*(1), 75–96. https://doi.org/10.1558/cj.29513

Kusyk, M., Arndt, H. L., Schwarz, M., Yibokou, K. S., Dressman, M., Sockett, G., & Toffoli, D. (2025). A scoping review of studies in informal second language learning: Trends in research published between 2000 and 2020. *System, 130*, 103541. https://doi.org/10.1016/j.system.2024.103541

Lai, C. (2017). *Autonomous language learning with technology beyond the classroom*. Bloomsbury Publishing.

Lai, C., & Gu, M. (2011). Self-regulated out-of-class language learning with technology. *Computer Assisted Language Learning, 24*(4), 317–335. https://doi.org/10.1080/09588221.2011.568417

Lai, C., Liu, Y., Hu, J., Benson, P., & Lyu, B. (2022). Association between the characteristics of out-of-class technology-mediated language experience and L2 vocabulary knowledge. *Language Learning & Technology, 26*(1), 1–24. https://doi.org/10125/73485

Lai, C., & Sundqvist, P. (2025). Research agenda: Synergizing in-class and out-of-class language learning with technology. *Language Teaching*, 1–22. https://doi.org/10.1017/S026144482500014X

Lai, C., & Wang, Q. (2024). Online informal learning of English and receptive vocabulary knowledge: Purpose matters. *ReCALL*, 1–17. https://doi.org/10.1017/S095834402400017X

Lai, C., & Wang, Q. (2025). Profiles of media use purpose in informal digital learning of English and their association with vocabulary knowledge. *Computer Assisted Language Learning*, 1–31. https://doi.org/10.1080/09588221.2025.2501705

Lai, C., Zhu, W., & Gong, G. (2015). Understanding the quality of out-of-class English learning. *TESOL Quarterly, 49*(2), 278–308. https://doi.org/10.1002/tesq.171

Lai, W. Y. W., & Lee, J. S. (2024). A systematic review of conversational AI tools in ELT: Publication trends, tools, research methods, learning outcomes, and antecedents. *Computers and Education: Artificial Intelligence, 7*, 1–18. https://doi.org/10.1016/j.caeai.2024.100291

Lamb, M. (2004). 'It depends on the students themselves': Independent language learning at an Indonesian state school. *Language, Culture and Curriculum, 17*(3), 229–245. https://doi.org/10.1080/07908310408666695

Lamb, M. (2007). The impact of school on EFL learning motivation: An Indonesian case study. *TESOL Quarterly, 41*(4), 757–780. https://doi.org/10.1002/j.1545-7249.2007.tb00102.x

Lamb, M. (2013). 'Your mum and dad can't teach you!': Constraints on agency among rural learners of English in the developing world. *Journal of Multilingual and Multicultural Development, 34*(1), 14–29. https://doi.org/10.1080/01434632.2012.697467

Larson, R., & Csikszentmihalyi, M. (2014). The experience sampling method. In M. Csikszentmihalyi (Ed.), *Flow and the foundations of positive psychology: The collected works of Mihaly Csikszentmihalyi* (pp. 21–34). Springer. https://doi.org/10.1007/978-94-017-9088-8_2

Lee, J. S. (2019). Quantity and diversity of informal digital learning of English. *Language Learning & Technology, 23*(1), 114–126. https://doi.org/10125/44675

Lee, J. S. (2020a). An emerging path to English in Korea: Informal digital learning of English. In M. Dressman & R. Sadler (Eds.), *The handbook of informal language learning* (pp. 289–302). Wiley-Blackwell.

Lee, J. S. (2020b). Informal digital learning of English and strategic competence for cross-cultural communication: Perception of varieties of English as a mediator. *ReCALL, 32*(1), 47–62. https://doi.org/10.1017/S0958344019000181

Lee, J. S. (2022a). *Informal digital learning of English: Research to practice.* Routledge.

Lee, J. S. (2022b). Evaluation of instruments for researching learners' LBC. In H. Reinders, C. Lai, & P. Sundqvist (Eds.), *The Routledge handbook of language learning and teaching beyond the classroom* (pp. 312–326). Routledge.

Lee, J. S. (2024). Fostering access to Global English(es) through informal digital learning, Presented at the 70th TEFLIN and the 17th CONAPLIN International Conference, Universitas Pendidikan Indonesia, West Java, Indonesia, October 24, 2024.

Lee, J. S. (2025). Innovation in language learning and teaching for social impact. In H. Nesi & P. Milin (Eds.), *International encyclopedia of language and linguistics* (3rd ed.). (pp. 1–5). Elsevier.

Lee, J. S., Chen, J., & Drajati, N. A. (2024). Informal digital learning of English and perceptions of using EIL materials: Attitude toward varieties of English as a mediator. *Journal of Multilingual and Multicultural Development, 45*(5), 1762–1777. https://doi.org/10.1080/01434632.2021.2021213

Lee, J. S., & Chik, A. (2025, July 11). Bringing informal language learning into formal education in Asian EFL contexts [Symposium session] 23rd AsiaTEFL International Conference, Education University of Hong Kong, Hong Kong, China.

Lee, J. S., & Chiu, M. M. (2023). Modeling EFL learners' willingness to communicate: The roles of face-to-face and digital L2 communication anxiety. *Annual Review of Applied Linguistics, 43*, 64–87. https://doi.org/10.1017/S0267190523000090

Lee, J. S., & Chiu, M. M. (2024). Modelling trait and state willingness to communicate in a second language: An experience sampling approach. *Studies in Second Language Learning and Teaching, 14*(3), 483–514. https://doi.org/10.14746/ssllt.37541

Lee, J. S., & Drajati, N. A. (2019a). English as an international language beyond the ELT classroom. *ELT Journal, 73*(4), 419–427. https://doi.org/10.1093/elt/ccz018

Lee, J. S., & Drajati, N. A. (2019b). Affective variables and informal digital learning of English: Keys to willingness to communicate in a second language. *Australasian Journal of Educational Technology, 35*(5), 168–182. https://doi.org/10.14742/ajet.5177

Lee, J. S., & Dressman, M. (2018). When IDLE hands make an English workshop: Informal digital learning of English and language proficiency. *TESOL Quarterly, 52,* 435–445. https://doi.org/10.1002/tesq.422

Lee, J. S., Kiaer, J., & Jeong, S. (2025). The role of informal digital learning of Korean in KFL students' willingness to communicate. *Journal of Multilingual and Multicultural Development, 46*(3), 863–879. https://doi.org/10.1080/01434632.2023.2216671

Lee, J. S., & Lee, K. (2021). The role of informal digital learning of English and L2 motivational self system in foreign language enjoyment. *British Journal of Educational Technology, 52*(1), 358–373. https://doi.org/10.1111/bjet.12955

Lee, J. S., Leung, R. T. Y., Drajati, N. A., Hidayati, M., Suhardi, D., & Seta, A. K. (2025, August 20–21). Enhancing speaking skills in access-limited communities: AI-mediated Informal Digital Learning of English (AI-IDLE). The 2nd EdUHK x HKUST Joint International Conference on AI and Education, EdUHK.

Lee, J. S., Liu, G., & Soyoof, A. (Eds.). (2026). Informal Digital Learning of English (IDLE) as innovative pedagogy: Mapping current and future trends. *Journal of Computer Assisted Learning.* https://onlinelibrary.wiley.com/page/journal/13652729/call-for-papers/si-2025-000977

Lee, J. S., & Lu, Y. (2023). L2 motivational self system and willingness to communicate in the classroom and extramural digital contexts. *Computer Assisted Language Learning, 36*(1–2), 126–148. https://doi.org/10.1080/09588221.2021.1901746

Lee, J. S., & Song, J. (2020). The impact of group composition and task design on foreign language learners' interactions in mobile-based intercultural exchanges. *ReCALL, 32*(1), 63–84. https://doi.org/10.1017/S0958344019000119

Lee, J. S., & Sylvén, L. K. (2021). The role of Informal Digital Learning of English in Korean and Swedish EFL learners' communication behavior. *British Journal of Educational Technology, 52*(3), 1279–1296. https://doi.org/10.1111/bjet.13082

Lee, J. S., & Taylor, T. (2024). Positive psychology constructs and Extramural English as predictors of primary school students' willingness to communicate. *Journal of Multilingual and Multicultural Development*, *45*(7), 2898–2916. https://doi.org/10.1080/01434632.2022.2079650

Lee, J. S., & Xie, Q. (2023). Profiling the affective characteristics of EFL learners' digital informal learning: A person-centered approach. *Innovation in Language Learning and Teaching*, *17*(3), 552–566. https://doi.org/10.1080/17501229.2022.2085713

Lee, J. S., Xie, Q., & Lee, K. (2024). Informal Digital Learning of English and L2 willingness to communicate: Roles of emotions, gender, and educational stage. *Journal of Multilingual and Multicultural Development*, *45*(2), 596–612. https://doi.org/10.1080/01434632.2021.1918699

Lee, J. S., Yeung, N. M., & Osburn, M. B. (2024). Foreign Language Enjoyment as a mediator between Informal Digital Learning of English and willingness to communicate: A sample of Hong Kong EFL secondary students. *Journal of Multilingual and Multicultural Development*, *45*(9), 3613–3631. https://doi.org/10.1080/01434632.2022.2112587

Lee, J. S., Zou, D., & Gu, M. (2024). *Technology and English language teaching in a changing world: A practical guide for teachers and teacher educators*. Palgrave Macmillan.

Lee, Y.-J. (2023). Language learning affordances of Instagram and TikTok. *Innovation in Language Learning and Teaching*, *17*(2), 408–423. https://doi.org/10.1080/17501229.2022.2051517

Li, M. (2018). Computer-mediated collaborative writing in L2 contexts: An analysis of empirical research. *Computer Assisted Language Learning*, *31*(8), 882–904. https://doi.org/10.1080/09588221.2018.1465981

Lin, J. (2023). The structural relationships among L2 motivation, out-of-class informal learning, and oral proficiency: A multiple-group structural equation modeling study. *Language Teaching Research*, 1–30. https://doi.org/10.1177/13621688231189030

Lin, T. J., & Lan, Y. J. (2015). Language learning in virtual reality environments: Past, present, and future. *Educational Technology & Society*, *18*(4), 486–497.

Liu, G. L., & Darvin, R. (2023). From rural China to the digital wilds: Negotiating digital repertoires to claim the right to speak. *TESOL Quarterly*, 1–29. https://doi.org/10.1002/tesq.3233

Liu, G. L., Darvin, R., & Ma, C. (2024a). Exploring AI-mediated informal digital learning of English (AI-IDLE): A mixed-method investigation of Chinese EFL learners' AI adoption and experiences. *Computer Assisted Language Learning*, 1–29. https://doi.org/10.1080/09588221.2024.2310288

Liu, G. L., Darvin, R., & Ma, C. (2024b). Unpacking the role of motivation and enjoyment in AI-mediated informal digital learning of English (AI-IDLE): A mixed-method investigation in the Chinese context. *Computers in Human Behavior*, *160*, 1–11. https://doi.org/10.1016/j.chb.2024.108362

Liu, G. L., Ma, C., Bao, J., & Liu, Z. (2023). Toward a model of informal digital learning of English and intercultural competence: A large-scale structural equation modeling approach. *Computer Assisted Language Learning*, 1–27. https://doi.org/10.1080/09588221.2023.2191652

Liu, G. L., Soyoof, A., Lee, J. S., & Zhang, L. J. (2025). Informal digital learning of English in Asian English as a foreign language contexts: A thematic review. *RELC Journal*, 1–8. https://doi.org/10.1177/00336882251332309

Liu, G. L., Zhang, Y., & Zhang, R. (2023). Bridging imagination and informal digital learning of English: A mixed-method investigation. *Journal of Multilingual and Multicultural Development*, 1–21. https://doi.org/10.1080/01434632.2023.2173214

Liu, G. L., Zhao, X., & Yang, B. (2024). The predictive effects of motivation, enjoyment, and self-efficacy on informal digital learning of LOTE: Evidence from French and German learners in China. *System*, *126*, 1–15. https://doi.org/10.1016/j.system.2024.103504

Liu, G. L., Zou, M. M., Soyoof, A., & Chiu, M. M. (2024). Untangling the relationship between AI-mediated informal digital learning of English (AI-IDLE), foreign language enjoyment and the ideal L2 self: Evidence from Chinese university EFL students. *European Journal of Education*, 1–12. https://doi.org/10.1111/ejed.12846

Liu, L., Guan, W. J., Qiu, Y., & Lee, J. S. (2024). Effects of extramural English activities on willingness to communicate: The role of teacher support for Chinese EFL students. *System*, *124*, 103319. https://doi.org/10.1016/j.system.2024.103319

Liu, L., & Lee, J. S. (2023). Why does IDLE make EFL learners gritty? The mediating role of enjoyment. In D. Toffoli, G. Sockett, & M. Kusyk (Eds.), *Language learning and leisure: Informal second language learning in the 21st century* (pp. 241–268). De Gruyter. https://doi.org/10.1515/9783110752441-011

Lomicka, L., & Ducate, L. (2021). Using technology, reflection, and noticing to promote intercultural learning during short-term study abroad. *Computer Assisted Language Learning*, *34*(1–2), 35–65. https://doi.org/10.1080/09588221.2019.1640746

MacIntyre, P. D., Gregersen, T., & Mercer, S. (2016). *Positive psychology in SLA*. Multilingual Matters.

Marks, B., Sisirak, J., & Chang, Y.-C. (2013). Efficacy of the HealthMatters Program train-the-trainer model. *Journal of Applied Research in Intellectual Disabilities*, *26*, 319–334. https://doi.org/10.1111/jar.12045

McCallum, L., & Tafazoli, D. (Eds.). (2024). *Computer-Assisted Language Learning in the Global South: Exploring challenges and opportunities for students and teachers*. Routledge.

Melnyk, B. M., & Morrison-Beedy, D. (2012). *Intervention research: Designing, conducting, analyzing, and funding*. Springer Publishing Company.

Mitra, S., Tooley, J., Inamdar, P., & Dixon, P. (2003). Improving English pronunciation: An automated instructional approach. *Information Technologies & International Development*, *1*(1), 75–84. https://doi.org/10.1162/itid.2003.1.1.75

Monk, R. (2005). *How to read Wittgenstein*. W.W. Norton.

Mortel, T. F. v. d. (2008). Faking it: Social desirability response bias in self-report research. *Australian Journal of Advanced Nursing*, *25*(4), 40–48.

Naghdipour, B. (2022). ICT-enabled informal learning in EFL writing. *Journal of Second Language Writing*, *56*, 100893. https://doi.org/10.1016/j.jslw.2022.100893

Nah, K. C., White, P., & Sussex, R. (2008). The potential of using a mobile phone to access the Internet for learning EFL listening skills within a Korean context. *ReCALL*, *20*(3), 331–347. https://doi.org/10.1017/S0958344008000633

Nexø, M. A., Kingod, N. R., Eshøj, S. H., Kjærulff, E. M., Nørgaard, O., & Andersen, T. H. (2024). The impact of train-the-trainer programs on the continued professional development of nurses: A systematic review. *BMC Medical Education*, *24*(30), 1–15. https://doi.org/10.1186/s12909-023-04998-4

Nielson, K. B. (2011). Self-study with language learning software in the workplace: What happens? *Language Learning & Technology*, *15*(3), 110–129.

Papi, M., & Hiver, P. (2025). Proactive language learning theory. *Language Learning*, *75*(1), 295–329. https://doi.org/10.1111/lang.12644

Park, J.-K. (2009). 'English fever' in South Korea: Its history and symptoms. *English Today, 25*(1), 50–57. https://doi.org/10.1017/S026607840900008X

Pearson, P. D., & Gallagher, M. C. (1983). The instruction of reading comprehension. *Contemporary Educational Psychology, 8*(3), 317–345. https://doi.org/10.1016/0361-476X(83)90019-X

Peng, H., Jager, S., & Lowie, W. (2021). Narrative review and meta-analysis of MALL research on L2 skills. *ReCALL, 33*(3), 278–295. https://doi.org/10.1017/S0958344020000221

Peng, H., Jager, S., & Lowie, W. (2022). A person-centred approach to L2 learners' informal mobile language learning. *Computer Assisted Language Learning, 35*(9), 2148–2169. https://doi.org/10.1080/09588221.2020.1868532

Peng, H., Lowie, W., & Jager, S. (2022). Unravelling the idiosyncrasy and commonality in L2 developmental processes: A time-series clustering methodology. *Applied Linguistics, 43*(5), 891–911. https://doi.org/10.1093/applin/amac011

Peng, L., Akhter, S., & Hashemifardnia, A. (2025). Podcast-integrated speaking instruction: Enhancing informal digital learning of English, academic engagement, and speaking skills. *Acta Psychologica, 258*, 105158. https://doi.org/10.1016/j.actpsy.2025.105158

Pennycook, A., & Makoni, S. (Eds.). (2019). *Innovations and challenges in applied linguistics from the Global South*. Routledge.

Prior, M. (2019). Elephants in the room: An "affective turn," or just feeling our way? *Modern Language Journal, 103*(2), 516–527. https://doi.org/10.1111/modl.12569

Razzouk, R., & Shute, V. (2012). What is design thinking and why is it important? *Review of Educational Research, 82*(3), 330–348. https://doi.org/10.3102/0034654312457429

Reinders, H., & Benson, P. (2017). Research agenda: Language learning beyond the classroom. *Language Teaching, 50*(4), 561–578. https://doi.org/10.1017/S0261444817000192

Reinders, H., Lai, C., & Sundqvist, P. (Eds.). (2022). *The Routledge handbook of language learning and teaching beyond the classroom*. Routledge.

Reinders, H., & Lee, B. J. (2023). Tracking learner engagement in the L2 classroom with experience sampling. *Research Methods in Applied Linguistics, 2*, 1–13. https://doi.org/10.1016/j.rmal.2023.100052

Reinders, H., Park, J.-K., & Lee, J. S. (Eds.). (2025). *Innovation in language learning and teaching: The case of Korea*. Palgrave Macmillan.

Research Excellence Framework. (2021). Panel criteria and working methods (2019/02). https://2021.ref.ac.uk/media/1450/ref-2019_02-panel-criteria-and-working-methods.pdf

Reynolds, B. L., & Teng, M. F. (2021). Incidental and informal vocabulary learning: Introduction to the special issue. *TESOL Journal, 12*(4), 1–7. https://doi.org/10.1002/tesj.642

Rezai, A. (2024). Informal digital learning of English in teachers: Development and validation of a scale. *ReCALL*, 1–16. https://doi.org/10.1017/S0958344024000247

Rezai, A., Ashkani, P., & Moradian, M. R. (2025). Is informal digital learning of English significantly correlated with online motivation for learning, online foreign language enjoyment, and telecollaborative foreign language anxiety? Evidence from higher education. *International Journal of Human-Computer Interaction*, 1–15. https://doi.org/10.1080/10447318.2024.2445102

Rezai, A., & Goodarzi, A. (2025). Exploring the nexus of informal digital learning of English and online self-regulated learning in EFL university contexts: Longitudinal insights. *Computers in Human Behavior Reports, 18*, 100666. https://doi.org/10.1016/j.chbr.2025.100666

Rezai, A., Goodarzi, A., & Liu, G. (2025). A comparative study of the effects of informal digital learning of English in extracurricular and extramural settings on reading comprehension: A multi-analysis study on Iranian university students. *Computer Assisted Language Learning*, 1–26. https://doi.org/10.1080/09588221.2025.2491708

Rezai, A., Soyoof, A., & Reynolds, B. L. (2024a). Informal digital learning of English and EFL teachers' job engagement: Exploring the mediating role of technological pedagogical content knowledge and digital competence. *System, 122*, 1–16. https://doi.org/10.1016/j.system.2024.103276

Rezai, A., Soyoof, A., & Reynolds, B. L. (2024b). Ecological factors affecting students' use of informal digital learning of English: EFL teachers' perceptions. *Teaching and Teacher Education, 145*, 1–11. https://doi.org/10.1016/j.tate.2024.104629

Rezai, A., Soyoof, A., & Reynolds, B. L. (2024c). Effectiveness of informal digital learning of English on EFL learners' vocabulary knowledge: A mixed-methods investigation. *Computer Assisted Language Learning*, 1–26. https://doi.org/10.1080/09588221.2024.2350419

Richards, J. C. (2015). The changing face of language learning: Learning beyond the classroom. *RELC Journal, 46*(1), 5–22. https://doi.org/10.1177/0033688214561621

Richards, J. C. (2020). Exploring emotions in language teaching. *RELC Journal, 53*(1), 225–239. https://doi.org/10.1177/0033688220927531

Rogers, E. M. (2003). *Diffusion of innovations.* Free Press.

Ruspini, E. (2002). *Introduction to longitudinal research.* Routledge.

Sato, M., & Cárcamo, B. (2024). Be(com)ing an educational researcher in the Global South (and beyond): A focus on the research-practice relationship. *Educational Researcher, 53*(6), 359–369. https://doi.org/10.3102/0013189X241231548

Sato, M., Loewen, S., & Pastushenkov, D. (2022). 'Who is my research for?': Researcher perceptions of the research-practice relationship. *Applied Linguistics, 43*, 625–652. https://doi.org/10.1093/applin/amab079

Sauro, S. (2017). Online fan practices and CALL. *CALICO Journal, 34*(2), 131–146. https://doi.org/10.1558/cj.33077

Sauro, S., & Zourou, K. (2019). What are the digital wilds? *Language Learning & Technology, 23*(1), 1–7. https://doi.org/10125/44666

Schurz, A., & Sundqvist, P. (2022). Connecting Extramural English with ELT: Teacher reports from Austria, Finland, France, and Sweden. *Applied Linguistics, 43*(5), 934–957. https://doi.org/10.1093/applin/amac013

Seo, Y. (2025). The role of home language environment and parental efforts in children's English development in an EFL context. *Journal of Multilingual and Multicultural Development, 46*(2), 273–287. https://doi.org/10.1080/01434632.2023.2177657

Smit, J. P., & Hessels, L. K. (2021). The production of scientific and societal value in research evaluation: A review of societal impact assessment methods. *Research Evaluation, 30*(3), 323–335. https://doi.org/10.1093/reseval/rvab002

Smith, B., Jiang, X., & Peters, R. (2024). The effectiveness of Duolingo in developing receptive and productive language knowledge and proficiency. *Language Learning & Technology, 28*(1), 1–26. https://hdl.handle.net/10125/73595

Sockett, G. (2014). *The online informal learning of English.* Palgrave Macmillan.

Sockett, G., & Toffoli, D. (2020). Last words: Naming, framing, and challenging the field. In M. Dressman & R. Sadler (Eds.), *The handbook of informal language learning.* Wiley-Blackwell.

Soyoof, A., Reynolds, B. L., Neumann, M. M., & Vazquez-Calvo, B. (2024). Maternal scaffolding of Iranian children's extramural Informal Digital Learning of English (IDLE): A qualitative study.

Early Childhood Education Journal, 1–17. https://doi.org/10.1007/s10643-024-01675-z

Soyoof, A., Reynolds, B. L., Vazquez-Calvo, B., & McLay, K. (2023). Informal digital learning of English (IDLE): A scoping review of what has been done and a look towards what is to come. *Computer Assisted Language Learning*, *36*(4), 608–640. https://doi.org/10.1080/09588221.2021.1936562

Stockwell, G. (2008). Investigating learner preparedness for and usage patterns of mobile learning. *ReCALL*, *20*(3), 253–270. https://doi.org/10.1017/S0958344008000232

Stockwell, G., & Wang, Y. (Eds.). (2025). *The Cambridge handbook of technology in language teaching and learning*. Cambridge University Press.

Sugimoto, C. R., Work, S., Larivière, V., & Haustein, S. (2017). Scholarly use of social media and altmetrics: A review of the literature. *Journal of the Association for Information Science and Technology*, *68*(9), 2037–2062. https://doi.org/10.1002/asi.23833ia

Sulistyawati, A. (2025, June 23). The 6th International Knowledge Transfer Forum Ulas Pembelajaran Bahasa Inggris. *Espos News*. https://news.espos.id/forum-di-ums-mengulas-pembelajaran-bahasa-inggris-berbasis-integrasi-idle-dan-ai-2110193

Sundqvist, P. (2009). *Extramural English matters: Out-of-school English and its impact on Swedish ninth graders' oral proficiency and vocabulary Karlstad University*. Karlstad.

Sundqvist, P. (2019). Commercial-off-the-shelf games in the digital wild and L2 learner vocabulary. *Language Learning & Technology*, *23*(1), 87–113. https://doi.org/10125/44674

Sundqvist, P. (2022). Learning across the lifespan: Age, language learning, and technology. In N. Ziegler & M. González-Lloret (Eds.), *The Routledge handbook of second language acquisition and technology* (pp. 343–355). Routledge. https://doi.org/10.4324/9781351117586-30

Sundqvist, P. (2024). Extramural English as an individual difference variable in L2 research: Methodology matters. *Annual Review of Applied Linguistics*, 1–13. https://doi.org/10.1017/S0267190524000072

Sundqvist, P., & Sylvén, L. K. (2016). *Extramural English in teaching and learning: From theory and research to practice*. Palgrave Macmillan.

Sundqvist, P., & Wikström, P. (2015). Out-of-school digital gameplay and in-school L2 English vocabulary outcomes. *System*, *51*, 65–76. https://doi.org/10.1016/j.system.2015.04.001

Sylvén, L. K., & Sundqvist, P. (2012). Gaming as extramural English L2 learning and L2 proficiency among young learners. *ReCALL, 24*(3), 302–321. https://doi.org/10.1017/S095834401200016X

Sylvén, L. K., & Sundqvist, P. (2017). Computer-Assisted Language Learning (CALL) in extracurricular/extramural contexts. *CALICO Journal, 34*(1), i–iv. https://doi.org/10.1558/cj.31822

Taherian, T., Shirvan, M. E., Yazdanmehr, E., Kruk, M., & Pawlak, M. (2023). A longitudinal analysis of informal digital learning of English, willingness to communicate and foreign language boredom: A latent change score mediation model. *The Asia-Pacific Education Researcher*, 1–14. https://doi.org/10.1007/s40299-023-00751-z

Tam, H. I., & Reynolds, B. L. (2022). The relationship between extramural English engagement and the vocabulary size of L2 Cantonese speakers in Macau. *International Journal of Applied Linguistics*, 1–35. https://doi.org/10.1075/itl.21003.tam

Tapscott, D. (1996). *The Digital Economy: Promise and peril in the age of networked intelligence*. McGraw Hill.

Tapscott, D. (2008). *Grown up digital: How the net generation is changing your world*. McGraw Hill.

Tao, J., & Xu, Y. (2022). Parental support for young learners' online learning of English in a Chinese primary school. *System, 105*, 1–12. https://doi.org/10.1016/j.system.2021.102718

Toetenel, L. (2014). Social networking: A collaborative open educational resource. *Computer Assisted Language Learning, 27*(2), 149–162. https://doi.org/10.1080/09588221.2013.818561

Toffler, A. (1980). *The third wave*. Bantam Books.

Toffoli, D. (2020). *Informal learning and institution-wide language provision: University language learners in the 21st century*. Palgrave Macmillan.

Toffoli, D., & Sockett, G. (2015). University teachers' perceptions of Online Informal Learning of English (OILE). *Computer Assisted Language Learning, 28*(1), 7–21. https://doi.org/10.1080/09588221.2013.776970

Toffoli, D., Sockett, G., & Kusyk, M. (2023). *Language learning and leisure: Informal second language learning in the 21st century*. De Gruyter Mouton.

Tsang, A. (2023). "The best way to learn a language is not to learn it!": Hedonism and insights into successful EFL learners' experiences in engagement with spoken (listening) and written (reading) input. *TESOL Quarterly, 57*(2), 511–536. https://doi.org/10.1002/tesq.3165

Tsang, A., & Lee, J. S. (2023). The making of proficient young FL speakers: The role of emotions, speaking motivation, and spoken input beyond the classroom. *System*, *115*, 1–10. https://doi.org/10.1016/j.system.2023.103047

UNICEF. (2020). Strengthening Digital Learning across Indonesia: A Study Brief.

University Grants Committee (2023 October). Research Assessment Exercise (RAE) 2026 Framework. www.ugc.edu.hk/doc/eng/ugc/rae/2026/framework.pdf

Uztosun, M. S., & Kök, M. (2023). L2 skill-specific anxiety and communication apprehension: The role of extramural English in the Turkish context. *Innovation in Language Learning and Teaching*. https://doi.org/10.1080/17501229.2023.2217170

Vazquez-Calvo, B., Zhang, L. T., Pascual, M., & Cassany, D. (2019). Fan translation of games, anime, and fanfiction. *Language Learning & Technology*, *23*(1), 49–71. https://doi.org/10125/44672

Warnby, M. (2022). Receptive academic vocabulary knowledge and extramural English involvement: Is there a correlation? *International Journal of Applied Linguistics*, *173*(1), 120–152. https://doi.org/10.1075/itl.21021.war

Warschauer, M. (2000). The changing global economy and the future of English teaching. *TESOL Quarterly*, *34*(3), 511–535.

Warschauer, M. (2003). *Technology and social inclusion: Rethinking the digital divide*. The MIT Press.

Warschauer, M. (2004). Technological change and the future of CALL. In S. Fotos & C. Brown (Eds.), *New perspectives on CALL for Second and Foreign Language Classrooms* (pp. 15–25). Lawrence Erlbaum Associates.

Wittgenstein, L. (1958). *Philosophical investigations*. Basil Blackwell Ltd.

Wouters, M., Bollansée, L., Prophète, E., & Peters, E. (2024). The relationship between extramural English and learners' listening comprehension, reading comprehension, motivation, and anxiety. *Vigo International Journal of Applied Linguistics*, *21*, 165–193. https://doi.org/10.35869/vial.v0i21.4570

Wu, H., & Wang, Y. (2025). Disclosing Chinese college students' flow experience in GenAI-assisted informal digital learning of English: A self-determination theory perspective. *Learning and Motivation*, *90*, 102134. https://doi.org/10.1016/j.lmot.2025.102134

Wu, R. (2023). The relationship between online learning self-efficacy, informal digital learning of English, and student engagement in online classes: The mediating role of social presence. *Frontiers in Psychology*, *14*, 1–14. https://doi.org/10.3389/fpsyg.2023.1266009

Yang, S., Xu, W., Liu, R., & Yu, Z. (2024). Influencing and moderating variables in informal digital learning of English through a structural equation model. *Computer Assisted Language Learning*, 1–36. https://doi.org/10.1080/09588221.2023.2280645

Yashima, T. (2002). Willingness to communicate in a second language: The Japanese EFL context. *Modern Language Journal*, *86*(i), 54–66. https://doi.org/10.1111/1540-4781.00136

Yiu, W. (2024, December 28). Hong Kong schools to receive HK$400,000 to boost schools' English and Mandarin learning. South China Morning Post. www.scmp.com/news/hong-kong/education/article/3292513/hong-kong-schools-receive-hk400000-boost-english-and-mandarin-learning?

Yu, S., Liu, C., & Zhang, L. (2023). Understanding L2 writers' lived experiences of informal writing: A phenomenological approach. *Journal of Second Language Writing*, *60*, 1–12. https://doi.org/10.1016/j.jslw.2023.100979

Yung, K. W.-H. (2015). Learning English in the shadows: Understanding Chinese learners' experiences of private tutoring. *TESOL Quarterly*, *49*(4), 707–732. https://doi.org/10.1002/tesq.193

Yung, K. W.-H. (2019). Exploring the L2 selves of senior secondary students in English private tutoring in Hong Kong. *System*, *80*, 120–133. https://doi.org/10.1016/j.system.2018.11.003

Zadorozhnyy, A., Lai, W., & Lee, J. S. (2024, July 4). Factors affecting IDLE integration into formal language education system: The case of in-service language teachers of Hong Kong, Technology-enhanced Language Learning and Teaching & Corpus-based Language Learning and Teaching (TeLLT & CoLLT), EdUHK, Hong Kong.

Zadorozhnyy, A., Lai, W. Y. W., & Lee, J. S. (2025). EFL teachers' ecological barriers to integrating informal digital learning of English. *TESOL Quarterly*, 1–26. https://doi.org/10.1002/tesq.3400

Zadorozhnyy, A., & Lee, J. S. (2023). Informal Digital Learning of English and willingness to communicate in a second language: Self-efficacy beliefs as a mediator. *Computer Assisted Language Learning*, 1–21. https://doi.org/10.1080/09588221.2023.2215279

Zadorozhnyy, A., & Lee, J. S. (2024). Linking EFL students' psychological needs to engagement in Informal Digital Learning of English: A structural equation modelling analysis. *Computer Assisted Language Learning*, 1–25. https://doi.org/10.1080/09588221.2024.2387269

Zadorozhnyy, A., & Lee, J. S. (2025). Comparing classroom and digital settings: The role of basic psychological needs on EFL students' IDLE engagement. *ReCALL*, 1–18. https://doi.org/10.1017/S0958344025000059

Zein, M. S. (2017). Elementary English education in Indonesia: Policy developments, current practices, and future prospects. *English Today*, *33*(1), 53–59. https://doi.org/10.1017/S0266078416000407

Zhang, R., Zou, D., Cheng, G., Xie, H., Wang, F. L., & Au, O. T. S. (2021). Target languages, types of activities, engagement, and effectiveness of extramural language learning. *PLoS ONE*, *16*(6), e0253431. https://doi.org/10.1371/journal.pone.0253431

Zhang, Y., & Liu, G. (2022). Revisiting informal digital learning of English (IDLE): A structural equation modeling approach in a university EFL context. *Computer Assisted Language Learning*, 1–33. https://doi.org/10.1080/09588221.2022.2134424

Zhang, Y., & Liu, G. (2023). Examining the impacts of learner backgrounds, proficiency level, and the use of digital devices on informal digital learning of English: An explanatory mixed-method study. *Computer Assisted Language Learning*, 1–28. https://doi.org/10.1080/09588221.2023.2267627

Zheng, Y., & Xiao, A. (2024). A structural equation model of online learning: Investigating self-efficacy, informal digital learning, self-regulated learning, and course satisfaction. *Frontiers in Psychology*, *14*(1276266), 1–18. https://doi.org/10.3389/fpsyg.2023.1276266

Zou, M. M., Liu, G., Li, D., & Chen, H. (2025). Beyond motivation: Modeling the predictive role of L2 pride in informal digital learning of English. *International Journal of Applied Linguistics*, 1–15. https://doi.org/10.1111/ijal.12738

Zou, M. M., Noughabi, M. A., Sabouri, M., & Zhou, L. (2025). The contribution of informal digital learning of English (IDLE) to achievement emotions and willingness to communicate: A cross-cultural investigation. *Journal of Multilingual and Multicultural Development*, 1–19. https://doi.org/10.1080/01434632.2025.2490076

Zou, M., Teng, M. F., Soyoof, A., & He, X. (2025). Informal Digital Learning of English (IDLE) as form-focused and meaning-focused activities: Refining its measurement and examining its predictive role in L2 achievement and confidence. *International Journal of Applied Linguistics*, 1–16. https://doi.org/10.1111/ijal.12781

Funding Acknowledgments

This work was supported by the EdUHK–RAE 2026 Development Impact Case Study (Grant #02212). Additional funding was provided partially by the General Research Fund (Grant #18605024) and the Standing Committee on Language Education and Research (SCOLAR) (Grant #1047-2050-8080-9020-00049).

Artificial Intelligence Statement

AI tools (Poe.com) were used sparingly to improve readability. All ideas and content remain entirely the author's own work.

Images in Figures 1, 2, and 5 were generated with the assistance of ChatGPT.

Cambridge Elements

Language Teaching

Heath Rose
University of Oxford

Heath Rose is Professor of Applied Linguistics at the University of Oxford and Deputy Director (People) of the Department of Education. Before moving into academia, Heath worked as a language teacher in Australia and Japan in both school and university contexts. He is author of numerous books, such as *Introducing Global Englishes*, *The Japanese Writing System*, *Data Collection Research Methods in Applied Linguistics*, and *Global Englishes for Language Teaching*.

Jim McKinley
University College London

Jim McKinley is Professor of Applied Linguistics at IOE Faculty of Education and Society, University College London. He has taught in higher education in the UK, Japan, Australia, and Uganda, as well as US schools. His research targets implications of globalization for L2 writing, language education, and higher education studies, particularly the teaching-research nexus and English medium instruction. Jim is co-author and co-editor of several books on research methods in applied linguistics. He is an Editor-in-Chief of the journal System.

Advisory Board

Gary Barkhuizen, *University of Auckland*
Marta Gonzalez-Lloret, *University of Hawaii*
Li Wei, *UCL Institute of Education*
Victoria Murphy, *University of Oxford*
Brian Paltridge, *University of Sydney*
Diane Pecorari, *Leeds University*
Christa Van der Walt, *Stellenbosch University*
Yongyan Zheng, *Fudan University*

About the Series

This Elements series aims to close the gap between researchers and practitioners by allying research with language teaching practices, in its exploration of research informed teaching, and teaching-informed research. The series builds upon a rich history of pedagogical research in its exploration of new insights within the field of language teaching.

Cambridge Elements

Language Teaching

Elements in the Series

Assessment for Language Teaching
Aek Phakiti and Constant Leung

Sociocultural Theory and Second Language Developmental Education
Matthew E. Poehner and James P. Lantolf

Language Learning beyond English: Learner Motivation in the Twenty-First Century
Ursula Lanvers

Extensive Reading
Jing Zhou

Willingness to Communicate in a Second Language
Jian E. Peng

Core Concepts in English for Specific Purposes
Helen Basturkmen

Teaching Second Language Academic Writing
Christine M. Tardy

Metacognition in Language Teaching
Mark Feng Teng

Data-Driven Learning In and Out of the Language Classroom
Pascual Perez-Paredes and Alex Boulton

Language Teacher Emotions
Juyoung Song and Elizabeth R. Miller

Content and Language Integrated Learning (CLIL)
Yolanda Ruiz de Zarobe

Informal Digital Learning of English
Ju Seong Lee

A full series listing is available at: www.cambridge.org/ELAT

For EU product safety concerns, contact us at Calle de José Abascal, 56–1°,
28003 Madrid, Spain or eugpsr@cambridge.org.

www.ingramcontent.com/pod-product-compliance
Lightning Source LLC
LaVergne TN
LVHW011853060526
838200LV00054B/4305